NO NONSENSE
LEADERSHIP

A REALISTIC APPROACH FOR
THE COMPANY OFFICER

FOREWORD BY DEPUTY CHIEF DAVE LEBLANC

JARROD SERGI

Copyright © 2019 Jarrod Sergi
Published by: Jarrod Sergi
Edited by: Krystal Barrad
Cover: Cassy Roop – Pinkinkdesigns.com

All rights reserved. No part of this publication may be reproduced, distributed, or transmitted in any form or by any means, including photocopying, recording, or other electronic or mechanical methods, without the prior written permission of the author.

ISBN: 9781700693402

ACKNOWLEDGEMENTS

I want to thank my beautiful and super supportive wife Gosia, and our two amazing boys, Max and Leo. You are the reason I take breath after breath and work so hard. Thank you for your unyielding support in the pursuit of my passion. I love you!

Thank you to my cousin Krystal for your advice and patience as I went from firefighter to author for a short period of time.

Thank you to all my mentors from the US Navy and the Fire Service. There are too many to list here, but you know who you are.

"A leader is a person who has not only the ability, but the willingness to achieve exceptional results through people."

Major Dick Winters

FOREWORD
BY DAVE LEBLANC

"The most powerful tool you have is your leadership example" – John Wooden

I have been fortunate enough to know Jarrod Sergi for several years and to call him a friend. When he reached out and asked if I would write this foreword, my first thought was he had texted the wrong number. I am honored and humbled to be asked.

Jarrod is an easy to get along with passionate firefighter who has developed an excellent presentation about leadership at the company officer level. "Fire Service Mortar" is Jarrod's take on leadership at the company officer level. Unlike many leadership talks, it is basically a script for how Jarrod operates as a company officer. It talks about what works and what doesn't. Jarrod's passion is evident in every class he teaches, and every conversation he has. He is clearly an asset to his department and the fire service.

Like most quality things in life, we know good leadership when we see it. We also know bad leadership when we see it. Unfortunately, leadership is not something the fire service spends a lot developing in its personnel.

I sat through a class put on by Chief Salka (FDNY Ret), and he asked the question, "What did your department do to prepare you to lead a company of firefighters?" The answers in the room varied, like it does in almost everything the fire service does. Some were sent to weeks of training and others were handed a badge and sent to a new firehouse. I mean after all, you did pass a test, and even did well enough to get promoted. What else could you possibly need? Unfortunately, most study materials fall far short of preparing us to become leaders.

If you think about you own career in the fire service, I am sure you can identify some great leaders that you have worked for, or even with. Yes with, because not all leaders will have rank. I am sure you can also remember some leaders that were not so good. Most of us, throughout our careers learned from both, we learned what to do and what not to do; we also adopted the traits of the good leaders for when our chance came to be in charge.

Anyone can be a leader. As with anything in life, some are born with natural talent and ability to lead other people, and others aren't. Naturally, those with strong ability will do better than those without, but this doesn't mean those without natural leadership ability can't become good leaders. They will just need help to get there. In either case, being a good effective leader, will require practice. Whether commanding a fire or addressing a personal issue, both require you put the effort in to become adept the challenges you will face.

How many can remember working for a good officer in the firehouse, only to have that same officer be a disaster on the fireground? Or vice versa? It is difficult to be good at everything, and some will struggle with being good at both. But you can be the best firefighter on the fireground, making the best decisions every time and still fail as a company officer when you get promoted, because no one ever took the time to develop your ability to lead people.

The fire department is all about people. We swear an oath to protect them and we must work with them to do so. As a company officer we must lead them. This isn't as easy as it sounds because people can be complicated, and we are not all the same. So, to be an effective leader, you must first understand your people. We don't all see things through the same lens and if we aren't clear about our expectations, then the roots of conflict start to take hold.

We all have flaws. There are things we can do better. Some of the best leaders in history had flaws. Often these caused them setbacks and issues within their commands. As a good leader, recognizing your flaws is a huge advantage to becoming effective. Self-awareness and focusing on the areas you are weak in only makes you more effective. As you read through this book, you won't see any fancy ideas or complicated metrics about how to be a good leader. There is no secret sauce contained within these pages, and no magic way to suddenly become the best leader the fire service has ever seen. What you will see is some time tested a proven guidance that is easy to understand and apply. Whether studying to be promoted, or a Chief officer, Jarrod's thoughts on leadership will help you become a better leader.

> "Look out for you people, and don't forget where you came from."

INTRODUCTION

Right after I graduated high school I was 18 years old and eager to go off into the world and do some growing up. My grandfather was a retired firefighter and my dad spent some time as a wildland firefighter in his younger days. I had just enough exposure at a younger age to take interest. A couple years before graduation I spent some time as an explorer with the local fire department. This is where I got my first taste of what firefighting had to offer. I was able to spend some time in the stations, respond on calls, and really see the firehouse dynamic and the clash of multiple personalities. No time was spent on a hose line or crawling down hallways, but it was here that I saw just what I wanted to be a part of. I had the opportunity to attend some week-long academies that the explorer post put on. During these academies we would not only practice firefighting skills, but also participate in several team building exercises.

I spent time as an explorer for the City of Hesperia. To this day I can still see those firefighters and the passion they had for the job, and just how much camaraderie they had amongst them. I grew up in Southern California in the Los Angeles and San Bernardino areas. It was not unusual for a fire department to require a paramedic certification to even apply to take the entrance exam. I was a young kid with not a whole lot of money so the idea of going to paramedic school was quickly taken off my table. What was my next best approach to enter the fire service?

A friend of mine told me about her brother recently joining the military and how he was really gaining a lot from it and also earning money for college. I heard exciting stories of jets, ships, travel and more. I thought to myself, why not? This may be the perfect opportunity for me to serve my country for a few years, earn some money for college, and get my professional career started. Sounds just like the commercials, right? I went down to the local recruiter to make an inquiry into the whole military thing. As I got out of the car I was in a strip mall. In this strip mall were all the offices for each branch of the military. I stood there for several minutes wondering which door I should walk through. I was looking at all of the posters that displayed the various jobs you may perform and all the catch phrases that went along with them. I caught the attention of a Navy recruiter returning from lunch and he quickly made his way over to me. He read me like a book and knew exactly why I was there. He said to me "so, you are here to look into the Navy huh? I said, "Sure I guess so", and off I went. To this day I believe that if it was a Marine recruiter that got to me first, I would be a Marine. If it was an Army recruiter I would be a soldier. If it was the Coast Guard recruiter, well, I would have probably still gone for the Navy. Just a little light humor for my Coast Guard friends.

There were a number of questions thrown my way, with one being,

"What would you like to do?"

I told him I wanted to be a firefighter.

"Have we got the job for you," he replied. "How about a Damage Control man?"

"Wow, Damage Control man, that sounds extreme—where do I sign?"

I went to boot camp, and like any 18 year old kid, was completely rattled by culture shock. I can remember sitting in the airport before heading out. You can always tell the group of young kids getting ready to go off to boot camp. We all have stone cold faces and carried around a big manila envelope that was to be delivered up arrival at your destination. I finally made it and was able to get through boot camp with no issues. The hardest thing for me about that experience was learning how to come together as a team in such a short time. Staying mission focused helped along with the occasional verbal assault from some of the company commanders. After completing boot camp, I was sent to Damage Control School which was just right down the street from where

I spent the last several months. Here I learned how to be a shipboard firefighter, as well as how to teach others to be firefighters. I learned all about how to save the ship from fires, flooding, and chemical weapon attacks. Upon completion of my school I was sent to the USS Iwo Jima (LHD-7) home ported out of Norfolk Virginia. Shortly after arriving one of my shipmates and I were sent off to be Search and Rescue Swimmers (SARs). This was probably one of the hardest things I have ever done. SAR School was physically and mentally demanding. It entailed miles upon miles of swimming and running over the next few months until we stood tall on graduation day. I had a great foundation to build upon at this point and I was eager to prove myself. And so, it had begun, the beginning of my leadership journey started as a wet-behind-the-ears sailor fresh out of boot camp, in a place I had never been, with a group of people I didn't know.

Some of these people that I worked for and with as an 18 year old kid still come into my head when I think about who influenced me to be the person I am today. There are a precious few who guided me and mentored me over the years as a young sailor. These men taught me my very first lesson in leadership: To be a good leader, I had to be a good follower. I was taught the importance of loyalty, mission, team, and accountability. One important thing that I learned as a follower was to know exactly what my leaders, my supervisors, expected of me. Expectations were the gateway for me to begin to perform the way I was supposed to and in the manner in which would support the team and mission. If you don't know what your leaders expect of you, find out. It is ultimately up to them to set those expectations for you, but if they are failing to do so, in a respectful manner, pry a little.

As a follower in the Navy I had the ability to look at a lot of different people. I saw the behavior of my peers, as well as my supervisors, and I saw how their behaviors impacted the team. Not only did I see how they impacted the team as a whole, but also how each action they took affected every person on an individual level. It was easy for me to see how people responded to different types of criticism, reinforcement, and counseling. You have to pay attention to those things as a follower. If you pay attention to how individuals are affected, you will be able to see what works and what doesn't. As a follower, identify the traits that fall under poor leadership. I have muttered under my breath several times that I wouldn't be like that guy or girl when I am in their position. It was here as a follower I started to cherry pick the positive leadership traits that I wanted to hold onto along the way and ultimately use when I found myself in a leadership position. If you are that follower right now, you should be doing the same thing. You should be identifying what you feel is important to bringing value to your team, your firehouse and your fire department.

The Navy didn't ask for leadership, it demanded it. I started off as the brand-new sailor that was left to grunt work and dirty details. I moved up the ranks and became a work center supervisor responsible for all firefighting equipment and training. After that I went across the hallway to be the supervisor of the fire protection systems shop. I left the Navy as the Leading Petty Officer of the division I served in. Here I was responsible for both work centers and twenty-two sailors. Twenty-two different personalities, needs, values, and opinions. I will be forever grateful that the US Navy provided me with a good leadership foundation at such a young age. I still think about all of my Officers, Chiefs, and fellow sailors that I served alongside. The military gets many things right. One in particular is developing and training leaders. There is no option in the military to not step up and be a leader. You either move up, or you move out. I was absolutely privileged to serve my country and took so much away from that experience. Go Navy!

After leaving the military I stayed in Norfolk, Virginia and was applying for many different fire departments in the area. I was lucky enough to get picked up right away with Norfolk Fire Rescue. Norfolk is a great place to work. It is an old busy east coast city that offers a lot of great experiences for a firefighter. I went through the fire academy and landed in a station shortly after. Just like my time in the Navy I was influenced by great people. The environment that I have grown up with in the fire department has always been one of high standards and accountability. The firefighters and officers I worked alongside were top notch and still are today. I came out of the fire academy and was sent to a station full of self-starters and motivated firefighters. People were eager to grab me and take me out to the apparatus bay and show me something. I had officers with credibility that led by example and were always there to teach me something or share an experience that would make me better. They were never too busy for me and always made the time, or took the time, to make my development the priority. I would like to think my probationary year as a firefighter was a successful one and I am grateful for all those guys who were with me at Station 7, you know who you are. The majority of my time as a firefighter was spent at Fire Station 2 before I was promoted. The firefighters I worked with were hard working, passionate, and believed in making our station and our department the best one in the state of Virginia. These men also helped shape the person I am today. Our Captain at station 2 was top shelf. When I hear someone talk about a top-notch Engine Company Officer, he is one of the ones that comes to mind. He showed us what the fire service was all about. He taught us about many fire service traditions. He showed us the importance of training and mission success. He led from the front and set the example. On top of all this he was extremely effective at engine company operations. I owe the trumpets on my collar today to this man. He did right by all of us, he prepared us. Not everyone has been fortunate to say they have worked for great officers or alongside top-notch firefighters. I was extremely lucky and will always be grateful. Let's face it, there are some terrible leaders out there and you may have had to work for one or may be working for one right now. This should light a fire under you even more to develop yourself as a great leader and inspire other firefighters around you to do the same. Every one of us can be shaped by our environment. Every one of us also has an individual responsibility to take ownership. In the absence of a good leader, someone has to step up. Let it be you. Don't ever use the excuse of, "Well I had a bad officer so I couldn't learn anything." Go out and get it!

I am currently serving as an Engine Company Captain and I have loved being a Company Officer. Not because I have my own room, or because it was a nice pay raise. I love it because I have the ability to take ownership over a crew and influence them in a positive way. There is something I live by as a company officer, call it an ethos if you will: If one of my firefighters is injured or killed in the line of duty, and I can't look their wife, husband, son, or daughter in the face and say I did everything I could to train them or increase their chance of survival, then I have failed. I refuse to let that happen to me. I refuse to let that happen to them. I understand the fire ground is a dangerous place. It is unpredictable at times and very dynamic. Bad things happen when everything goes right at a fire. I share this ethos or mindset with my crew very early. By them knowing and understanding my mindset they will never have to question where my decision-making process is coming from. Everything I do will be in their best interest and in the best interest of the team as a whole. If you are a company officer and this is not at the front of your brain every day you report for duty, shame on you. Your firefighters are the most important people in that station. Not you, not your part time job, nothing. In that time spent at the station, they are number one and you should be acting like it.

I have had the fortunate opportunity to travel all over the country and talk about the need for strong company level leadership. This book contains content from that program and if you have sat through one of my courses, this will all sound very familiar. This short book is meant to inspire you to take action wherever you sit in your career. I certainly don't have all the answers. I haven't been around this fire service for 25 or 30 years. My goal with the advice offered in this book is to simply share with you what has worked for me both in the military and the fire department when it comes to building teams and a strong company. My intent is not to bore you with leadership theory and throw you a bunch of hypotheticals. My intent is to share with you realistic and practical ways to be an effective company officer. This is clearly not the first book out there on leadership. I am not an inventor of anything new out there nor am I some pioneer in the way we lead people. Everything you read and the approaches that I take are because I have had good mentors in my corner. This leadership journey is a constant learning process for me. I succeed, I fail, I regret decisions at times, but I stand behind most. I really want to target those who are currently in that position as a company officer, or those looking to step into the role. If you are not a company officer, that is ok. This book will still give you tools today to take action tomorrow. We need strong leadership at all levels, but when it's not there, it better be, it must be, the company officer that holds your organization together. Here is how we do it…

CHAPTER 1
GET READY FOR THE TRUMPETS

"Before you are a leader, success is all about growing yourself. When you become a leader, success is all about growing others." -Jack Welch

So, all that studying has paid off and your new collar brass is ready to come out of the little plastic bag to be placed on your collar. It is a pretty exciting time for you and it should be. To me, there seems to be a honeymoon phase soon after a promotion. You are excited that all your hard work has paid off and there are many congratulations flooding your way. It's not long before the honeymoon is over and the real responsibility creeps up on you. Those who have prepared themselves long before this happens will be ready to see the challenges and rewards that come along with their responsibility. Those who have not will struggle along the way.

Long before those trumpets are placed on your collar, and even before you were sitting down for your written test, your credibility as a leader has been building. I truly believe that good company officers start out as good firefighters. They are passionate about their profession and are committed to being efficient at their craft. I still look at a company officer as a firefighter. By that I mean, they are on the line and need to stay engaged in firefighting tasks such as ventilation, hose stretches (of all sorts), search and rescue, EMS care, and more. It's these tasks that you will later have to teach your firefighters when you are their leader. Confidence follows competence and if they can't count on you to lead by example, you will struggle as a leader.

One of the most important roles a company officer will play is that of an instructor. To be an effective instructor you must invest in your development, because when you put those trumpets on it is no longer about you; it is about your crew and what you will be able to provide for them. If no time was invested into this position you are about to step into, or are already in, you will be behind in so many ways and your people will see right through you. So, ask yourself,

- What am I doing now to prepare for tomorrow?
- Am I taking classes and attending conferences?
- Am I participating in firehouse drills?
- Am I the firefighter who I would want to come get my family out if they were trapped?
- Am I truly preparing for the role of the company officer?

It totally fries my ass that there are so many out there who will invest time, money, and energy into competing for the promotional exam only to let those trumpets tarnish when given a promotion. They sit in their bunk room or office all day long, they fail to mentor, they fail to teach, fail to lead. I have one word for it, negligence. These are likely the same people have failed to develop themselves and produce for the people around them as well as their department. Why these types of folks are rewarded with promotions is beyond me. The bottom line is this, if we put people in leadership positions that have failed to develop themselves along the way, we shouldn't be surprised when they fail to develop others. Sometimes the problems we scratch our heads over can truly be seen coming from a mile away. We have to break this cycle of unprofessional development and reward people that produce for their firefighters, their stations, and their departments. Credible leaders have built a path paved with a blend of competence and execution of the above-mentioned tasks. Be the kind of company officer that can make a company great! Be that officer that people will want to follow because they know that you can bring out the best in them. You have this ability because you have prepared and are ready to lead with passion and purpose, for them.

I am almost certain everyone reading this book can rattle off a few traits that make a great company officer. I want to share with you the ones that are near and dear to me and elaborate on each one. These are traits that

I pulled from the leaders I had in the military and the fire service, as well as traits that the firefighters I worked alongside displayed.

HAVE A POSITIVE ATTITUDE

It is truly amazing to witness just how powerful a positive attitude is. You must continually display a positive attitude in front of your crew. Are there going to be days when it may seem hard to pick yourself up out of the office chair or head out to the drill ground? Absolutely, but you are the leader! You now must lead from the front and a positive attitude is infectious. I have seen the environment in a station do a complete 180 simply because that officer had a great attitude. They were positive and excited about training, they shared their passion with their crews and you knew without a doubt that they loved this job even when it got tough. Even in the face of adversity they did not let it overpower their need and obligation to maintain a positive attitude in their firehouse. Why? Because the power of positivity is immeasurable and coupled with this next trait it can make amazing things happen in your firehouse.

LEAD BY EXAMPLE

This seems like it should go without saying, but often times this doesn't happen. Leading by example can be a difficult thing. Some say it's easy, but some days I am not so sure. You should never ask your crew to do something you won't do or haven't already done. If you want them to get in shape, you better be in shape. If you want them to look professional, you better look even better. If you expect them to go out and develop their career, you better have done the same thing when you were in their shoes. If you lead by example you set the tone for the rest to follow. Your example is everything and if you fail to lead by example, people will see right through you. It is easy to sit on the sidelines with arms crossed; anyone can do that. Don't just be a spectator. Get on the ground with them. Crawl down the hallway yourself. Just because you are the instructor doesn't mean you can't jump in the shoes of the student as well. After all, aren't we all students of this fire service? That doesn't change when those trumpets are on your collar. In fact, I would argue that it comes with an obligation to do more.

EXUDE COMPETENCE

Lest face it, confidence follows competence. We are going to talk a lot about trust throughout this book and it's because your firefighters must trust you. Competence can come in many forms over many subjects, but the bottom line is people want to follow and work for someone who knows what the hell they are doing. This doesn't magically happen once you get your pay raise. This starts long before you sharpen the pencil for that promotional exam. In the book *The Mental Game of Baseball* the author describes two types of ball players, good ones and great ones. The good ones will show up on game day and give their best for the team. The great ones have their heads in the game long before they see their first pitch or dive for that fast grounder. They train, study their opponents, take countless hours of batting practice, and more. They spend most of their time in the preparation phase and not just the execution. Firefighters should be no different. Aspiring company officers need to prepare for game day. They need to prepare for that right front seat. Strategy and tactics, leadership, evaluations, and the down and dirty firemanship type stuff will prepare them for that role. Don't just be a good company officer, be a great one. Your crew needs you to be!

BE DECISIVE

Teddy Roosevelt once said: "In any moment of decision, the best thing you can do is the right thing, the next best thing you can do is the wrong thing, and the worst thing you can do is nothing." Just make a decision. Now, don't just make a decision for the sake of making one, make one based on logic, facts, and the circumstances that present to you at that time. People want to follow a leader who will make a decision even if after the fact it may not have been the best one. If your crew members ask something of you and you have the answer and the authority, make the decision in the best interest of the crew and the station. If a company officer has to pick up the phone and call their chief about every single decision they make, there are two things I see here. One, you have a micromanaging chief, or two, you are afraid to just make a damn decision. For the most part I have always been a beg for forgiveness (not permission) type of guy. That has gotten me into trouble on occasion but more times than not it has gone well, thanks to just making the call and handling it. You're the officer for a reason; be decisive. If you are making the best decision with the information you have at the moment, and it is being done with the public, your crew, and the department in mind, most times you can't go wrong.

BE A GOOD MANAGER

There is certainly a big difference between leadership and management. I am not going to break them both down, but a good leader needs to also be a good manager. You have, or will have, administrative responsibilities as well. You need to be able to manage your time, your personnel, training calendars, recertification hours, and more. You must stay organized as a company officer. In my opinion one of the biggest things you have to manage as a company officer is your time. Depending on the size of the station you may have a lot on your plate. You may have 10 things you need to accomplish that day and if you don't get yourself organized and manage your time well, things get missed. Being a good leader is essential, but knowing how to manage people, time, and other administrative responsibilities is also essential.

ACTIVELY LISTEN

This is something that I am still working on and struggle with myself. I think it's important that we take the time to truly listen to our people. Shut the phone down, kill the computer screen, and shut off the TV. I am talking about actively listening to what our people have to say. And I am not talking about just the stuff that's easy to hear or the things where you can pull a solution off the shelf and the problem is solved. I am talking about the gripes, the complaints, and the not-so-pretty stuff. Listen to what people have to say and pay attention. Take notes, follow-up, and remember important days. For example, I had a firefighter who was very close to his mother and she passed away. It was Mother's Day the next year and I knew it would be a rough one for him. I knew this because I LISTENED to him whenever he would talk about her. That Mother's Day I called him up and said, "Hey man, I know it's a tough day for you because you were so close to your mom and I just wanted to say I was thinking about you, Brother." Give a damn about people and listen to what is going on in their lives. Listen to what drives them, pisses them off, and hone in on their suggestions. Allow them to open up to you without fear of judgement or reprimand. Being a good listener builds trust and that is the key ingredient to this whole leadership game.

SHOW YOU ARE TRUSTWORTHY

Your men and women have to trust you. They. Have. To. Trust. You. There are many ways to earn people's trust and we will talk about a few of them throughout these pages. They must know that you will be willing and able to take care of uniform requests, on up to competent (there is that word again) decision making on the fire ground, and everything in between. A foundation of trust is built upon your ability to say and do the right thing. The moment there is no trust, there is no team. Be the type of leader your people can count on. Be the type of leader who builds trust and is careful with it once you have it.

I am sure there are dozens of other traits out there that make a great leader and a great company officer. As I said before, I have gathered these watching some of the leaders that I had and still have great respect for. I have also kept my eyes on the bad ones. Sometimes I have many thanks to give the bad leaders I have seen along the way. They make the learning process so easy. I essentially just watch what they do and then do the opposite.

Now that we have discussed all those important traits, I want to close this chapter out talking about values. Having a specific set of values can really drive the direction of your decision making. It is important to have your own set of values because as you move through your career, they will help you gather your thoughts, your words, and your actions. They will determine how you handle certain situations and the outcomes of many challenges you may face. Most organizations have their own set of values and I am sure your fire department is no different. I can remember several years back we had a committee get together to discuss what our core values would be in my department. Around 8-10 people locked themselves in a room and finally landed on a set for the department. Ours are pretty easy to remember and all are important.

They are as follows:
-Accountability
-Integrity
-Respect
-Professionalism
-Safety
-Innovation

Now let's remember, these are organizational values. What about your personal values? The values above should be ones that every employee aspires to, right? Core values are great and should have some meaning. Like most places I have seen in my travels the laminated flyer with the core values almost always hangs near the minimum wage chart and the OSHA and Federal regulations charts in a spot that no one ever pays attention to. These organizational values should be the foundation for many things your organizations face every day. Service delivery, hiring's, promotions, counseling's, etc. Core values are just hollow words on your corkboards if you don't give them meaning. If we are going to post them all over our firehouses and refer to them in fancy graduation speeches or city council meetings, we better remember they have some substance. Nothing is worse than a leader spewing core values only to spit on them with their actions. If we can't follow through, just take them down. You may be checking the box on organizational leadership algorithm, but they will mean nothing.

So, let's talk about your personal values, which certainly may align with some or all of your organizational ones, but you own them. They are personal to you and have been developed over the course of your life. Maybe the environment you grew up in, the way your mother or father treated you, the mentors and friends in your life helped shape yours, and they likely did. These values will serve as your north star when you find yourself in conflict. These north stars will help you stay true to your beliefs and help you do what's right. As a company officer your set of values will directly impact the people who are in that firehouse. Naturally what is important to you will translate into your personal values and if you have never really thought about them I challenge you to do so. I have my own personal values and I will share them with you:

- Accountability
- Respect
- Professionalism

- Teamwork
- Trust

These are the values that are important to me as a company officer. I took a class in college and the professor was explaining what's called the Galatea effect to us. I am certainly no college professor and not always the best student, but I will do my best to explain. Essentially what this means is that our images, beliefs, and ideas about ourselves have a very powerful influence on our behavior. So, the bottom line is your values are reflected in your performance. What you value will become important to you, and it must be important to you first before it can become important for your crew. Let me just give you one personal example. I value physical fitness and staying ready to perform. It is all part of professionalism. When I reported to the station as a new Captain I can remember telling my crew that I wanted them and expected them to get at least 20 minutes of exercise a day. One day we went out for a run at a local track and I told everyone they could run, fast walk, or really do whatever exercise they wanted. As I was running around the track I could see one or two guys just casually strolling at a snail's pace. I started to become a little frustrated with this as I was circling the track and literally running circles around them. Once it looked like everyone was about done and our 20-30 minute time slot came to a close I got everyone on the front bumper and told them what I expected of them when it came to P.T. I was clear that if we were going to be out doing exercises like this we would not be out here just wasting time and they had better do something to at least get their heart rate up. One person looked at me like I was crazy and just kind of shrugged it off. I continued to explain my expectations about fitness and being ready over the months that would pass, as did a couple other people in the firehouse. This person knew that it was important to me and continued to see this is something that his officer valued. Today, that same person has transformed his mindset on physical fitness and we laugh about the incident at the track that day. He now values the importance of physical fitness and has seen the benefits. This is just one small example and you may have some of your own. The point is you must have values as an officer and those values need to be expressed verbally at times, but most importantly in your actions every single day you walk into that firehouse.

Just remember that the honeymoon phase we covered earlier is great but will eventually wear off and the reality of your responsibility should set in. Those nice shiny trumpets and the excitement of a promotion will soon come to reality and you will feel, or at least should feel, the weight of those trumpets on your collar. Remember the traits that you looked for in a good company officer and try to emulate those. Keep a set of values to help drive good decision making that will allow you to take good care of your folks. Take this role seriously! Your crew needs you!

CHAPTER 2
YOUR NEW ROLE

"When you become a leader, you give up the right to think about yourself." -Gerald Brooks

In my opinion there are many things that the military gets right almost daily. The one thing that stands out to me is the way they develop their leaders. I am not taking anything away from a guy/girl who wants to ride the back step their whole career. In fact, I would say that we need strong senior firefighters to lead by example and coach and mentor in the absence of good company officer leadership. In the military this simply wasn't an option. The military demanded leadership. This stems from a long history of conflict and battlefield promotions where it was critical to know how to do your job, and know the guys below and above as well. This demand for leadership led to an understanding that there was no such thing as minimum standards. There was no room for mediocrity and your crew members needed your best all the time. Every branch may be a little different, so I can only speak to the Navy, but I will explain to you how they did this. First, they had what we would call in the fire service an officer development program. As an enlisted guy once I was promoted to E-4 I went to a leadership program that focused on that specific rank and what would be required of me. The same thing when I was promoted to E-5. I once again sat through a program and was taught by my peers on what will be expected of me in that position. The class isn't enough though. While it was beneficial, the cherry on top was the mentorship that came from other senior petty officers and chiefs. They made it a point to grab you and take you aside to offer guidance and leadership advice. They believed in the power of good mentors and made sure they were going to leave a legacy in their wake to carry on a proud naval tradition of outstanding leadership. The core values of the Navy, honor, courage, and commitment meant something to them. Lastly, there was tough love. They we very hard on me at times and were always honest, even if I didn't want to hear it. I always admire the leader who can wear many hats of leadership. The ones in the military seem to do it well. They care enough about you to look out for you, even if it means being a little harsh. I will always be grateful to those folks who showed me not only what a leader should be, but being hard on me as well, even if I didn't want it.

On the warship Iwo-Jima it was not uncommon for me to hear two principles repeatedly, especially around promotion time. They would come up in conversation about mentorship and really reinforced after a bump in pay grade. In the Navy there is, or was, a tradition of "tacking on the crow." A newly promoted petty officer would have an eagle with hash marks placed on their left sleeve. The eagle was black on your work uniform so we just called it a crow. Many people thought that the low budget thread used to sew this patch on your sleeve just wasn't enough, or it was just a fun opportunity to blast your arm with all they got. What would happen as you moved through the passageways was other petty officers and some chiefs would walk up, shake your hand, and punch your left arm to "tack on the crow." I can remember looking at my arm after the first few days and it was all kinds of interesting colors from the abuse. Black and blue, yellow and purple, to the point where I could barely move it. I am almost confident that doesn't take place any more. The thing I remember most about all those right hooks I took to my arm is what people would tell me after they did it. They would give me their best punch, shake my hand and say "Just remember these two things: look out for your people and don't forget where you came from." Over and over again I would hear this. That has stuck with me and I try to apply these two golden principles of leadership in all that I do in the firehouse. I have been extremely fortunate in my career to be surrounded by some pretty amazing people. Not everyone has had that. Officer development programs are great, but in the absence of good mentorship, in the absence of a formal officer development program, if you do these two things, you are more than halfway there as far as I am concerned. By applying these two principles into the majority of your decision making you can and will be an effective company officer. Now just remember, if you are stepping into this new role, or have been in it already for some time, remember this: You are a walking, talking, living, breathing officer development program. People are watching you and paying attention to every move you make. Be the type of leader people need! Be the type of leader that maybe you didn't have when you were climbing the ladder. Create an environment where people can realize their potential and what they have to offer to the team and the organization.

Let's quickly break each one of these principles down.

LOOK OUT FOR YOUR PEOPLE

This is done in many ways. Sadly, I have seen firefighters want to go work for an officer that "looks out for his guys" only to see the reason is for it his lack of accountability, structure, training, and more. They like working for this officer because he "lets them do whatever they want." This is not looking out for your people. This is negligence. Looking out for your people means keeping their best interest in mind. It means focusing on their development and holding them to a high standard. Mix a little bit of accountability in there and you have the right recipe for success. Army General Bruce Clarke once said, "You owe it to your men to require standards which are for their benefit even if they may not be popular at the time." I often try to remember what the general said here. I can remember as a firefighter my captain held us to very high standards. There were plenty of times where I wondered if he would ever crack; he didn't. I don't think I truly appreciated what he was doing and did for us until I was later promoted. It's almost scary how much I find myself doing the same things he did for me. Accountability is often viewed as a bad thing, it's not. Accountability grabs outliers who are getting off track and moves them back toward that path to excellence, back toward that standard you have set. I tell all my firefighters, "I will back you up all the way if you are right but will hold you accountable when you are wrong."

REMEMBER WHERE YOU COME FROM

Never forgetting where you came from comes down to empathy. I am not talking about the empathy where you own every firefighter's emotions as your own and make irrational decisions. I am talking about understanding what emotions they may be feeling and combining logic to make an educated decision. Always consider the view from the other person's lens. When you are sitting down to give an evaluation remember how your evaluations used to go. Were they good or bad? How was the body language of the officer? Remember how you felt when someone was talking to you about your performance, good or bad. When your firefighters come to you with issues or problems think about how you were treated when you brought up the same issues years ago. Think about how your previous leadership led training. Was it productive or hollow? Were they passionate or just checking a box on their quarterly reports? One of the biggest gripes I used to hear in the military and still do to this day is officers forgot where they came from. I think with movement up the ranks this happens even though people may not want it to. Don't allow that to happen to you. How many times have you said to yourself "If I was in that position I would do this…"? Remember that feeling when you are actually there and you will ensure you never forget where you came from.

There is no greater privilege than the privilege to lead people. Every single day when you cross the threshold of that firehouse your firefighters are at the top of your priority list, right next to the mission of the fire department. It drives me absolutely crazy that there are company officers out there who spend time and money to go through a process only to disregard their responsibilities when they get them. The only time you spot them is when it's time to eat or when the brass hits for a call. There is absolutely no place in our fire service for absent or negligent company officers. We decided the day we put those trumpets on our collars to place others above ourselves, like it or not. Every day we come to work we need to stand upon a set of values or principles. There has to be a driving force inside every one of us. I will share with you mine. If I was ever placed in a situation where one of my firefighters was seriously injured or killed in the line of duty and I can't look their spouse, brother, or child in the face and tell them I did everything I possibly could to ensure they went home, then I have failed. I will rest my head at night knowing that I put the firefighters under my command first and their welfare and development are my top priority. Bad things happen in this job that are beyond our control, and I get that, but if I can get ahead of anything and make my firefighters "hard to kill" as Major Jason Brezler says, then I have done my job. So again, I ask you, what will be your driving force? How will you honor your responsibility and how will you bring meaning to those trumpets? In addition to these two important principles there a few other things to keep in mind.

BE YOURSELF

I think there is pressure on a newly promoted officer where they feel like sometimes there must be this instant change in their personality. Just be yourself. Now, I am not saying there isn't a little decorum that comes with being an officer, but it should not change you as a person, especially if you have strong values and work ethic already. In fact, having these as a firefighter before promotion will make the transition that much easier. Far too often I have seen newly promoted officers act like a completely different person once that brass ends up on their collar. These are often the ones that are excommunicated from the rest of the team. I have received criticism for getting too close to my crew. We hear all the time in our profession that we have to go from buddy to boss. Not all the time. I think it is ok to be someone's friend at work. We need to be the boss, but sometimes we just need to offer friendship as well. This can obviously lead to problems if not tempered. If you find you cannot give honest criticism or a fair evaluation, it may be time to ask yourself if the friendship is getting in the way of your ability to be the boss. At one time I was stationed with my best man and one of my groomsman. I had to be mature enough to realize that our friendships were still friendships, but also know when to put the hat of a supervisor on my head.

DON'T BE AFRAID TO SAY I DON'T KNOW

There is more credibility in saying I don't know than you might think. Firefighters are very good at seeing right through people and knowing when you are a hollow leader. It is far better to just say I don't know than it is to blindly navigate a problem or make a completely uneducated decision. When I was promoted to Lieutenant I was assigned to a ladder company. I spent all my time on an engine company prior to this. I love engine work, I was confident in my abilities as an engine guy, and let's face it, the Engine Company is the center of the fire department universe so I was totally fine with that. In my department Lieutenants are assigned to ladders and Captain on engines. I probably went to a handful of fires on a ladder truck while filling in at other stations. All my experience was on the engine, and my firefighters knew that. It would have been foolish for me to go to that station and try to act like I was an experienced ladder firefighter. I had to work at it. So, I found myself saying "I don't know" quite a bit. "Hey Lieutenant, if we get the order to vent the roof how should we run it?" "If we get the task for primary search what tools do you want me to grab?" These are questions I would get and I could have said "Well, based off my experience we can do this," but I didn't have that well of experience to draw from. So, my response was often, "I don't really know, but how do you think we can make it happen efficiently?" That did a couple of things. One, it let that crew know I wasn't trying to just wing it. Two, I included them in the process of how we could improve operations. Ultimately, I took the advice of the crew members and my driver and we drilled on many things all the time. Doing that made us a very effective ladder company and I would like to think that this approach made us all better and I left that station as an ok ladder guy. I was off to my Engine Company.

NEVER PRE-JUDGE YOUR CREW

When you get your first assignment as an officer and really any other assignment to follow, pre-judging your crew is one of the worst things you can do. When I got my assignment as a new Captain it was not the assignment that was anywhere near the top of my list. When other members found out I was going there they pumped me full of all kinds of information about the station and the crew. I heard they are all lazy, didn't care about anything, don't like to train, and wouldn't listen or buy into anything I was going to try and do over there. I could have easily listened to that and walked in my first day with that information and it would have been disastrous! I didn't. Everyone gets a fresh start with me. When I hear people or a crew described that way it begs the question. Why? Why are they described that way? Poor judgement, false perception, or maybe they really are that way. I needed to find that out for myself and you know what I found? I found that most everything I heard was not true. Were there some challenges in the station? Sure there were. There was some immediate corrective action and interruption of behavior that had to happen. I found that by not pre-judging that crew and going in with a positive attitude and a good example I was able to work on building a team. I found a crew that was open to learning and training and even got to the point where they were self-sustainable and led training themselves. I found a crew that was happy coming to work and had positive attitudes. I have a crew now that is better today than they were when I got there. This is not all on me. I simply provided them with a roadmap on how to make themselves better. And truly, they have also helped me to be a better officer. This was no magic trick. No crazy science of management stuff. It was simple, I gave a damn. I gave a damn they were there and I gave a damn about where I wanted to take them as a team. Everything goes back to the leader, Always!

So, what should be some goals for you as a new officer? I am sure you will have some things you want to accomplish, but here is what I shoot for in my station and hope to leave when I walk away.

WELL TRAINED

I really believe in the value of training and have seen it pay off many times at incidents. Ultimately, I want my crew members to be able to go out and perform their jobs and provide the best level of service that they can. I will elaborate more later on what specifically I do when it comes to training and how to make it effective and realistic.

TAKE OWNERSHIP

I want them to take ownership in everything that they do. I don't care if it's from the dishwasher on up to the apparatus. If we see a problem, we own it and we fix it. I don't care if we just got back after a few days off and the B shift (sorry B shift) didn't take care of the problem. If we know about, and we can square it away, it's our problem now. Not just equipment or station items either, I want them to take ownership of their actions, their attitudes, their performance, and their role in the station as a member of a team. I will rally ownership by empowering them to make decisions and allowing them to fail forward.

THE CREWS HANDLE PROBLEMS AT THE LOWEST LEVEL.

I am a big believer in firefighters policing themselves. Don't get me wrong here, there are some things that should absolutely be passed up the chain of command, but sometimes what the Captain don't know, won't hurt the Captain. I want them to police themselves and manage conflict at their level for a specific purpose. If they choose to promote down the road, they are used to handling problems and resolving conflict. Also, when a problem does arise they don't need to pick up the phone and call the chief every time an issue comes up. I am not a chief, but I can imagine many times my chief or any chief thinking to themselves, you know, we pay you a decent wage to make decisions, take care of your firehouse. I had a guy storm into my office one time and was very upset about the probationary guy working out while everyone was washing the truck. He barreled in and said "that damn rookie is out there getting a workout in while we are washing the trucks. I paused for a moment and said, you guessed it, "what have you done about it?' He replied almost confused and said, well nothing you're the officer I figured you would want to know. I was ok with him informing me, but what needed to happen and what did happen was he addressed the problem first as his peer and senior firefighter and go from there. I am obviously there to help, but we need to encourage resolving conflict at the lowest level possible. If this is the way you manage you also have to pay close attention to how they manage their conflict. You may have to intervene, coach, or offer advice at times so it's done the right way.

DON'T FEEL YOUR ABSENCE WHEN YOU LEAVE

This can be both short term and long term. In the short term, I want and expect my firefighters to continue the tempo I have created for them when I am on leave or off for whatever reason. They are able to make sound decisions and remember the expectations I have laid out for them. In the long term, I hope they do the same when I leave. Let's spend some time on the latter for a moment. I have heard people say and even have read quotes along the lines of, a true measure of your leadership will be present when you are no longer there. That essentially your effectiveness as a leader will be measured based of the behavior and results those firefighters produce when you are no longer there to lead and coach them. Of course, we all want to leave a positive impact and legacy, but it is unfair at times to point the finger at the leader. This is obviously my opinion, but I think that can be a very unfair thing, based off the personalities that that leader was working with. Let's put this into context. You are a newly promoted officer, or maybe you have been an officer for some time. You find yourself in a station with some firefighters that have poor attitudes, subpar performance and more. While you are there you focus on building relationships, developing trust, train them the way you should and get them to a point where they feed off of your motivation and enthusiasm. You have what you would consider a great thing going with that crew. As their officer you have poured your heart and soul into them as you should. Now it's time to transfer and you head somewhere else. That crew that fed off of you for some time goes back to their old ways, they disengage in training and maybe they even have an officer who is the exact opposite of you and doesn't share the same level of commitment or expectation. That's your fault, right? You are a bad leader, right? Wrong, at least not in my book. It is so personality dependent when it comes to lasting impacts an officer can make. Strive to make them better every day, but understand people are all different and sometimes are simply a product of an environment that you create. Some will stick with it, some won't. That is just the reality.

HIGH MORALE

Crew morale is important to me and there are many ways to achieve it. I will keep this one short and sweet. You have an immense amount of control over your crew. There is no such thing as a morale chief and I would stress that morale can me improved much better by folks in a firehouse than by the people in headquarters. Unit cohesion is the ultimate killer of low morale. If you focus on creating a close tight knit cohesive team, high morale is a byproduct. How do you create cohesion? Work hard together, communicate openly, show appreciation for your people, socialize on and off duty, and stay mission focused.

Now let's move into Chapter Three and really talk about getting to know the folks who are under your command.

CHAPTER 3
SIZE-UPS

"Leaders must be close enough to relate to others but far enough ahead to motivate them."
-John Maxwell

One of the many things a Company Officer must be good at is sizing up buildings. This is an extremely important part of your job and like anything else takes practice and dedication. We will look at a building and try to figure out what type of construction it is or the building materials that were used. We want to know how that building will handle stress or behave under fire conditions. If it collapses was it something we should have seen coming or did it catch us by surprise. Even worse, have we totally neglected our size up and know nothing about the structure when a problem occurs. Often, I hear that we must be students of the craft and of our service. I totally agree with that. I also think we, especially company officers, need to be students of people. We need to understand emotions, opinions, and values. So, are you spending time sizing up your people? What inspires and motivates them, or what angers and frustrates them? Do you know about their family and hobbies? Before I went to my new assignment as a Ladder Lieutenant I was talking with my Chief at the time. I was telling him how excited I was to get back out to a company (I was coming from the training division) and how I was looking forward to the station life again and catching some fires. He chuckled a little bit and quickly said to me, "The fires will come, but your main job as a company officer is not going to be fighting fires, it going to be dealing with people." How right he was. I really think this is the key element missing from most officer development programs. Simply how to build relationships and focus on people.

I got my first taste of dealing with many different personalities in the Navy. As I became a supervisor, I was quickly learning about how to motivate and inspire others. I had people in my work center that were from all over the country. Different family values, political views, work ethic, and varying opinions on a wide array of topics. I had to figure out how to take all these different types of people and build a team. A firehouse is no different. One thing I have found to yield positive results is to truly get to know your people. People want to work for a leader who has a genuine interest in their success as well as a genuine interest in who they are as a human being. So, let's get all touchy-feely shall we?

When I got to my assignment as both a Lieutenant

and a Captain, I really wanted to study the people that were in my station. That process is certainly ongoing, but I really needed to nail it down within the first few months if I wanted to help build a team. I went out to my local big box store and grabbed myself a cheap notebook. I am sure if the people that were assigned to my stations are reading this, they may think it a little creepy. It just might be but stay with me here. I took the notebook to work with me and inside of it everyone had a page. In my department we have a program where I can see basic information about someone such as how long they have been employed, their address, training courses, etc. I would write all this stuff down in my notebook. Let's use Tom for this example. If I was out at the grocery store or around the galley table or even just a part of some conversation on the bay floor I would listen intently to Tom. I would pay attention to his wife's name if he mentioned it. I would want to know what he did for a part-time gig and what hobbies he may have. If Tom was having a conversation about his previous leadership, I would want to know all about how that experience was for him, good and bad. As soon as I got all this information in my head, I would go write it down on Tom's page. I did the same for every one of the people in that station, including the two other officers that were there with me. After all, we must be able to lead to our left, right and above us as well, not just down the chain of command. I didn't spend hours on end looking through all of this information, but I made sure that on occasion I would take a look at it and try to remember little details about this person and what they were made of. I wanted to know all of these little details because I needed to know what type of leadership style to use and when to use it. There is no cookie cutter out there for good leadership. You will have to change you approach at times and knowing your people will allow you to choose the right path.

You must show a genuine interest in the lives of your men and women, and trust me, they will know if its genuine or totally a façade. Building relationships in your firehouse is an essential part of earning trust and should be one of your first priorities as an officer. If you think for one second that just because you have gold on your back you will instantly get respect, you are wrong. It doesn't work that way. The gold letters on your back only make you look like an officer; it's your actions that will define you as one. People want to know that you have their best interest in mind. I was in my EFO program at the National Fire Academy and one of my classmates was explaining how we have to peel people back like an onion and study their different layers. I thought that was a pretty good analogy and I have also found that people tend to work in layers, or at least they are built in layers and just like learning how that building is constructed, we need to do the same with our firefighters. Depending on their personality type and where they are at in their career will dictate what layer goes where and really even what layers may exist. Let's break down what I am talking about here for a few minutes.

The following is an example of one type of person and how their layers may be broken down.

Station Tasks
Career
Hobbies
Personal Life
Family

The bottom layer is the stuff that people usually keep very close to them. They aren't usually going to open to you about this lower layer unless you have really established some trust and are building that relationship. You can see family is at the bottom of the example. As we move up, we can see that personal life comes into play. This could be what they do part-time, how they spend their days off, and other non-work-related things that affect their daily lives. As we continue to move to the surface, we see their hobbies. Maybe they like to play golf, fish, build model airplanes, or fly drones. All of this is still important for you to know. Then we start to get to the surface where some of these things are in your control, or at least they are things that you can influence. Their career layer might be their aspiration to be a company officer themselves one day, or a driver/operator, or a paramedic. At the very top of these layers are the things you have control over every single day you are in the firehouse. These can be task books for driving or acting officer and maybe even the training of your new probationary firefighter. So, let's say you walk up to that new probationary firefighter and tell him or her you are going to grab them later that day and show them how to stretch some lines off the truck or talk some fire behavior. Then that day comes and goes and you just don't get to it, and so does the day after that, and the day after that. It's now a brand-new shift and you go up to someone else who has a book to work on or something else you are supposed to help them with and they count on you to be there to help get it done, but you brush it off like you did with the new firefighter. Then one day you are browsing social media and see one of these guys or gals took a recent trip with their family out of town somewhere. You walk up to them and say, "Hey, I saw the pictures of you and your family on a trip a couple days ago. Did you have fun? How have your wife and kids been by the way?" What might they say to you and what might they be thinking. They might just humor you with a generic response, but I can bet they were thinking, you don't even care to take care of the things on the surface. You can't even dedicate 30 minutes to my professional development, so what makes you think I am going to let you reach down into that deep layer and let you into what goes on with my family. I have seen it. I have seen people totally closed off because an officer failed to care about them while they were at work and failed to make their training and career development a priority. I have also seen this chart flipped upside-down.

There are firefighters who expect you to know about their family. Their spouse's names, kids' names, etc. They want you to know that getting them home to their family is important. If they know you care about that, then they will trust you with the rest.

Part of your size-up also includes understanding the strengths and weaknesses of your crew members. You don't figure this out by making assumptions. You do it by paying attention. It would be unrealistic for you to expect the same level of performance out of every single person every single day. You need to understand what each person can contribute to the team. If you want to be let down, walk into your firehouse today and expect everyone to perform on the same level. That is simply not the case. I have also heard many times "they need to keep their personal life outside of work." While I agree with that to a point, there has to be an understanding that what goes on in people's personal lives can affect their job performance. What kind of officer, what kind of leader would I be if I didn't take that into consideration? A very hollow one. If I had a member of my firehouse who just had a close family member die, is going through a divorce, or is battling depression, I must be in tune to that. I first need to know that it is going on, so I can provide support, but also, I need to know mentally where that person is when the bell hits for a call. Just because *you* wouldn't respond or act a certain way doesn't mean they won't. We are all human beings who feel emotion and handle stress in different ways.

Maybe you have someone in your firehouse right now who could be considered lazy, apathetic, or disengaged. Why is that? Have you spent much time trying to figure out why this person is that way? Sadly, it's not uncommon for me to hear someone described a lazy or apathetic firefighter and when asked, "Well why do you think they are like that?" I hear, "That's just Joe, he's been that way for a long time." It is played off as the norm and frankly the acceptable behavior of that person. There is always more to it than that. Did they clash with their previous crew? Was there a personality conflict? Don't be so quick to count people out. Are there folks out there who frankly come to work and collect a paycheck? Of course, we can't save them all, but make sure we spend the time getting down to the root cause of people's behavior. Doing a good size-up will help you get there.

So, let me continue on with exploring people as individuals. Yes, you have a team to work with and manage, but each one of those team members can be very different. I want to to share my approach on how I treat different types of individuals, specifically, the two groups that are performers and non-performers. It could be described as a bit taboo and may not fall in line with the last leadership book you read, or the last speaker you listened to. Ever heard someone say "that's my go-to guy/girl"? I have. We all have ours I'm sure. Ever hear anyone say "You can't play favorites with your people"? I have heard that as well, and I have got to be honest, I totally disagree with that. I was listening to a podcast several months back and it was an episode with one of my former Chief Petty Officers who was talking about leadership. The whole podcast was really good, but one particular moment stood out to me. The person asking the Chief the questions said "Do you think it's wrong for leaders or supervisors to play favorites?" His response was great. He said "Absolutely not! I have my favorites. My favorites are the ones who show up early every day and are all in. They are the ones who are mission focused and keep their heads in the game. They mentor and train younger sailors. My favorites are the ones who take on extra responsibility when they don't have to and they are the ones that I can count on to get the job done." Hearing that was such a breath of fresh air for me. For the longest time I had always felt the same as the chief, but would never really say anything because, well, that's not what leaders do right? I shared the same approach as the Chief when I was in the military supervising other sailors. I was always hesitant to tell people I did that because I figured that made me a bad supervisor, a bad leader. Looking back now, I think I made some mistakes in the way I treated some of my higher performers. I was just under the impression that everyone shared the same consequence regardless of their performance. I will tell you right now that I absolutely play favorites amongst my team members. I even make sure that I am dedicating a lot of my time and energy into working with high performers because I know they are the ones who will go out there and produce for the team and the organization as a whole. I will even handle mistakes differently for them. Let me be very clear here at this point. Playing favorites is fine by me; however, it needs to be based off of work ethic, merit, and overall attitude and performance. Simply playing favorites with someone because of a personal relationship or because maybe you go back several years in the organization is wrong. It must be based off *merit* alone. I mentioned that I will even handout different punishment if needed. The rules will always apply to everyone, it's the consequences that I believe you should have to adjust. If you treated one of your problem folks the same way you did your top performers, you may end of with a result you didn't anticipate and that is dropping the productivity of that high performer. I believe that consequence isn't always so black and white. I think as an officer you have to be able to see things in shades of gray. So, don't sweep a broad brush and treat everyone exactly the same, treat them fair based off their work ethic, attitude, and results they produce for the team.

Let's take a look at two different people for just a moment and for a second place yourself in the shoes of the top performer. First though, let's talk about our non-performer who we will simply call Bill. There are a whole host of negatives I can tell you about Bill. He is a terrible relief in the morning. You know, the two minute till types. He takes no ownership, abuses sick leave, been late on several occasions, has customer complaints, shirks responsibility and lacks professionalism overall.

Then there is Mark. He is basically the opposite of

Bill. He is a self-starter, leads training, takes on additional work, mentors new people, motivated, competent and trusted by his peers and supervisors. Mark is pretty much the type of guy you want to clone and spread throughout your department. Now, rules apply to both of these guys, but you think if Mark happens to show up late one morning I am going to give him the same punishment as Bill? Not me, I am not doing that. I am not going to do that to Mark. Someone mentioned to me one day that they look at it like money in the bank. Marks account is full and can afford to get a withdrawal here and there. Bill is steady into overdraft because of his performance. I want to continue to see a high performance out of Mark so why would he be given the same consequences as Bill? I can list a dozen other examples and infractions, but the point is, be careful on how you dish out consequence. Are you still in Marks shoes? Now think of how you would feel if you saw I treated you the same way as the person who does the exact opposite of you. That may drive down your motivation and lead you to question why you try so hard when everyone gets treated the same anyway. Treat people fair! Now Bill may see that as unfair too and that's ok, because its justified. If Bill wants to feel a different consequence, if Bill wants to be one of the favorites, Bill has the ability to turn his performance around and produce for the team and the organization. So, you will have to help Bill you figure out what drives him. What are his specific drivers of high performance. What will make him get there?

Sizing your people up is extremely important and is an important first step in building relationships in your firehouse. I have found that there are many ways to build a successful team. Building relationships and still treating them as individuals is one of those key elements. In fact, the time you take to build those relationships will pay dividends later. Build relationships based on trust and understanding. Keep your core values at the foundation as well as the values of others. So, just as you would pre-plan a structure, figure out where the first line goes, and where to start your search, you must do the same with your people. Take the time to truly get to know them. They will see you have a genuine interest in doing so, and will be more likely to buy in to what you are trying to do in your firehouse. I bet if we were to ask all the Fortune 500 companies what their most valuable asset is, they would say their people. I would argue that the fire service is no different. There is no one-size-fits-all leadership strategy. Size up your people and work relentlessly to build those relationships. It will pay dividends later.

CHAPTER 4
EXPECTATIONS

"People can't live up to the expectations they don't know have been set for them"
-Rory Vaden

I AM A BIG BELIEVER IN SETTING expectations with my crew. I think this is something that a company officer must do early when getting their new assignment. There are many ways to deliver your expectations to your crew. I would offer to you that you should really get to feel out the personality types in your firehouse before you do this. We just talked about sizing people up and really getting to know them. This requires time and we don't always have the luxury of time when it comes to setting these expectations. This should be done early into your arrival of your new assignment. You can go into detail on what you expect on calls, duties around the firehouse, and what you want to see on the fireground and EMS scene. The crew should also know what to expect from you. Before

I even talk about what I expect from the crew I believe it is critically important for them to understand where I am coming from. It is important for me that they know where the foundation of all my decision making comes from. The first day, the very first day, when I reported as both a Lieutenant and as a Captain I shared the exact same thing. I told my crew members that my goal as their officer was to add value to the team. They could expect me to come to work with them being my priority every single shift and that the decisions I make will always be in their best interest. I went on to explain to them that they could expect me to always hold myself to a high standard and that I would also hold them to a high standard as well. As a Lieutenant I was assigned to a ladder and as a Captain I am assigned to an Engine. I told my crew that our company will be the best ladder or engine in the battalion, the best in the shift, and what the hell, why not the best in the whole department? With this being explained to them it removed all doubt of where I was taking that crew and the behavior they could expect from me. They now understood the roots of my decision-making process.

One thing I think is very important here is in the way you will deliver these expectations. When I arrived at my station as a new lieutenant, I had a crew that was middle of the road when it came to tenure. I would say the average time in service was around 10 years or so. Most of these members were high energy and you can almost feel that they wanted to see what they were going to get out of their new lieutenant. I could sense that I needed to lay out expectations very early on, what I wanted when it came to my ladder truck, and some other things around the station. It was received very well by them because of the types of personalities that were there. When I reported as a Captain to my new assignment, I was the baby. For the most part I was the guy with the least amount of time and my crews average time in the fire department was around 20 years. Had I taken that same approach I did with a younger crew, it would not have been well received. I still needed to deliver my expectation even if they all had 30 years, but it was all in the delivery and how I sent the message. The first day as a Captain I did have the conversation about me wanting to add value to the team and letting them know about the roots of my decision-making process. At that moment that was all they needed to hear. They knew they had a new Captain who cared about their wellbeing, set high standards for himself, and would always work with their best interest in mind. Just by doing this, they knew what types of behaviors and actions I would expect out of them. I didn't get into specifics, but that was enough for the moment. A few weeks went by and I studied their personalities, their interactions with each other and watched how things went on calls. After line-up one day I made a fresh pot of coffee and I asked if they would join me in the galley. We all got our cup of joe, sat down at the table, and I explained to them exactly this: "Things have been going really well here and I just wanted to cover a few more things that we haven't really gotten a chance to talk about. Expectations to me are very important and I feel like if I don't lay some of those out in front of you, then I have failed as your officer. It is important to me that I never put you all in that position." There were no tense shoulders, no apprehension, there was a casual conversation in detail about things that I expected to see from uniform appearance all the way up to actions on the incident scene. I think it was very well received. Had I gone in there from day one and said look here guys this is what I expect with force in my voice, I stood the chance of losing them. I didn't want that to happen, so I had to create a casual environment of trust where I could lay those out. I had to really understand that the way I deliver expectations to one crew cannot be the same way for another. It falls on you to understand the dynamic of people and personalities to know when the time is right and when those expectations will best be absorbed.

There is a whole lot of detail that you can get into when it comes to your expectations. You can elaborate on what you want to see with the rigs, the stations, behavior on calls, riding assignments, and much more. They are your expectations not mine, so pick the ones you are passionate about and believe are necessary for strong teams and team performance. Mine can be summed up into four items. These are four simple pillars that, when expressed to your crew, should capture the lion's share of your expectations as a Company Officer:

- Be ready
- Look professional
- Act professional
- Take care of each other

These are very simple expectations, but really cover a broad spectrum. Let's break down each one of these individually to really get a good look.

BE READY

This goes from mindset all the way up to execution. When you come through the doors of the firehouse your members need to be locked on and engaged! Their landscaping side work, real estate meetings, or other part-time responsibilities are important, but not as important as what they just showed up to do. When at the firehouse, they need to BE at the firehouse. Being ready also includes the condition of their apparatus. Every spanner wrench, crosslay, and SCBA should be ready to go immediately. If it not that way, we fix it. We don't blame it on the C shift (always the troublemakers). We take ownership of that rig and do what needs to be done.

Having their gear staged and ready to turnout quickly is also important. It is no good balled up in the back of the rig, or what's even worse, still in the locker nowhere close to the trucks. When you return from a call, its back into staged gear ready to do it all over again. Seconds add up. Seconds save lives.

Training and physical fitness also fall under this category. Having a well-trained crew should be a priority for so many reasons. It fosters unit cohesion, builds efficiency, and leads to positive outcomes on the incident scene. You crew members need to know that training is valuable and should expect a consistent training program while you are there. Keeping themselves in good physical condition, coupled with a consistent training regimen can only lead to success. They may be able to talk their way through a high-rise fire, but if they can't make it to the upper floors what good are they? Always be ready!

LOOK PROFESSIONAL

Uniform appearance is a big deal for me. We are professional public servants and we need to look the part. Walking into someone's home with a poor looking uniform appearance only shows lack of pride. Your firefighters should be proud of the department they serve: its history, its record of service, and what it does for the community. They should also be prideful in the company they work out of. I don't care if it's the busiest house or the slowest house, it's THEIR house, and they should be darn proud of what they can bring to the table. So, when they walk into the grocery store, city hall, or Mrs. Smith's living room, they should have the appearance that they take pride in who and what they represent. Maybe it's the military in me - I expect uniforms to always be squared away, but there must be give and take. My crew knows that during the day shirts are tucked in and we look like professionals on calls and in the firehouse. In the late afternoon or after dinner if they want to pull their t-shirts out of their pants and dress down a little bit, that is fine with me. I want them to be able to unwind and do that, but when the brass hits, we square away that uniform and head out the door. We look just as professional at 2 in the morning as we do at 2 in the afternoon. Call me petty, but a uniform appearance can tell me a lot about a person and just how much they care.

ACT PROFESSIONAL

Just because we look the part doesn't mean we're out of the woods. Your firefighters need to act the part as well. After all, we are professionals, right? This comes down to what behavior is allowed to take place in the firehouse on up to the way they converse with and treat the public. Once again there is an image to uphold. Your firefighters need to know what boundaries are in place and when they can push them. Far too many problems could have been fixed before they grew out of control. It only takes a little accountability and a few difficult conversations. Most big problems didn't start out that way. They were allowed to fester for too long because there was no line in the sand, no expectations. There was a boss who decided to look the other way instead of just being a boss. Their interaction with the public should be positive and productive. We have all been there when a patient has really pushed our buttons. Your firefighters need to know that as soon as they lose their cool, they lose all together. They should remain in control of their emotions and be the calm during the storm. Be that level headed professional. There are three things every one of us must consider when making a decision:

1.) Is this good for the public?
2.) Is this good for the department?
3.) Is this good for my station?

If that decision is going to have a negative impact on any of those three things, we better be very sure about what we are about to do and be ready to answer for the decisions we make. It amazes me how many millions of dollars in lawsuits and how much public trust has been lost in our fire departments simply because we didn't act like professionals. Even worse, a company officer somewhere knew about it and failed to get ahead of it. Don't be that guy/girl. Forecast problems, have the hard conversation, and make sure your people act professional.

TAKE CARE OF EACH OTHER

This one is so simple, but so important. Just take care of each other. That's it. Just look out for one another. I think we forget just how much we count on each other to get this job done. We are a team and we should act like one. We don't talk behind each other's back in the firehouse.

Your crew members need to know that you require an environment where problems are brought to the surface and handled at the lowest level possible. Your crew needs to understand that you want them to be a phone call away if something comes up off duty. We pride ourselves on words like family and brotherhood. We shouldn't just toss those words around so gently. Ensure your crew knows how much you care about them. I tell my crew all the time that I am here for them. My job as their company officer is round-the-clock. Your crew should be able to pick up the phone and call anyone on that shift roster without the first words out of their mouth being "I hate to bug you, but." If this idea of family and cohesion is important to you, it will be important to them. We have to take care of each other.

With just these four expectations you will be able to tackle so many questions that may be raised about the decisions you make.

- *Why do I have to get a new duty shirt, Captain?*

  Because I expect you to look professional.
- *Why are we going out and training today, Lieutenant?*

  Because I expect us to be ready.
- *How come you just didn't tell that patient what you really thought, Man?*

  Because we are professionals.
- *Why are we all in this room talking about this?*

  Because we take care of each other.

Expectations are a must and you set the tone as the Company Officer. I use every opportunity I can to revisit these expectations. If I have to counsel someone, they will hear them. If I must have a group meeting about an issue, they will hear them. I also use the annual performance review as another opportunity for my firefighters to hear them. Set your crew members up for success. If they go out the door and make a bad call and you haven't done this, you share in the blame. If you have, then there will be some level of accountability because you made them aware. I hope these four simple things can help keep your firehouse running as a well-oiled cohesive machine. They can be communicated quickly, with easy explanation, and the power of expectations can be immense. I mentioned the Galatea effect earlier and to really prove to you I was paying attention in class I will tell you about another effect known as the Pygmalion Effect. Again, I will do my best to explain. This is where you place high expectations on someone and in return they perform well. Basically, the higher the expectation, the better the work they perform. This effect was originally studied in teachers and their interactions with their students. The firehouse isn't much different than that classroom. The more you expect people to perform well, the more they will. If you expect nothing from them, guess what you get in return? When you put faith in your people and their abilities, with the right amount of mentorship and these expectations, there will be some increase in their self-esteem and hopefully a marked improvement in performance.

So, the final piece of this chapter is this: What do you expect from me? This should come after you laid out everything for your crew. Accountability and expectations work both ways. Ask your firefighters what they expect from you. Pay attention, take notes, and make sure you live up to their expectations as well, after all you are just as much a part of the team as they are.

CHAPTER 5
BUILDING YOUR TEAM

"Build for your team a feeling of oneness, of dependence on one another and of strength to be derived by unity."
-Vince Lombardi

Ever since I was 18 years old and throughout my career, I have been a part of a team. Not once in my adult professional life did my actions not have an impact on someone else, the team, or the organization as a whole. From being a young sailor up until now I have tried my best to pay attention to the successful ingredients of a team as well as what tears teams apart. From the smallest detail to the biggest issues, I have made it my personal mission to always find out what I can do to ensure that the team I am a part of is a successful one.

I believe there are five key pillars on which all successful teams are built. These pillars should hold the majority of your focus when working to build an effective team under your command. They are as follows:

1. Trust
2. Accountability
3. Communication
4. Sense of Purpose
5. Appreciation

So, let's break each one down just a little bit.

TRUST

All of the key pillars are important, but without trust there is really nothing else. Your firefighters need to be able to trust you as their company officer. From being able to take care of their basic needs such as uniforms and equipment on up to the critical decisions that you will make on the fireground or EMS scene. Let's face it, what you have done up to this point will play a factor. Confidence follows competence and if they know you have a credible history of being proficient at your job as a firefighter, that raises the level of trust they will have in you as an officer. You still have to prove your worth as their officer, but this certainly helps things.

One of the first ways to develop trust within your company is to show them that you truly value them. The decisions you make in the firehouse should have their wellbeing at the center of it. They need to see that you are focused on their professional growth, that you take the time to actively listen to their problems and show a genuine interest in getting to know them and building a relationship with them. Secondly, they need to see consistency out of you. Nothing is worse than working for a supervisor where you never know what you are going to get when you walk through the door. They need to see consistency in all things. Daily routines, counseling, discipline when needed, and most important your attitude. Another thing you need to be doing is asking what your firefighters think. Let them know you want to hear from them when it comes to a variety of topics. When a problem arises, and they bring it to your attention, one simple question can empower them and also show that you trust them as well, after all this works both ways right? That question is: What do you recommend? Ask them and listen to what they have to say. By doing this it shows them they are a part of the team, they have some say in what happens around here, and you want to hear want they have to say. Just because you are the officer, doesn't mean you have to make all the decisions. Give some of the work back to your crews and let them run with it while you just sit back and support them. Lastly, do what you say and uphold your promises and commitments. If you tell one of your firefighters that you are going to help him, then make sure you follow through. If you have a guy who is working on an acting company officer book and you tell him that you will work with him to get it done, dive right in. What I mean by that is focus on your commitment to them. Manage your time appropriately to ensure that you can focus on him/her. If all they keep hearing is empty promises and lack of follow through, they will lose confidence and trust, and will likely seek it out elsewhere if you are unable. There must be very little space between what you say and what you do. The more distance you put between those two things the more you stand to damage any trust you are trying to build. There are a number of things you will be focusing on when building your teams but building trust should be the highest priority.

ACCOUNTABILITY

The next pillar is accountability. Unfortunately, when people hear this word it is often associated with some form of discipline and that is not always the case. Accountability comes in many forms with the first one being holding people accountable to the standards and expectations that you have laid out for them. In the previous chapter we talked about expectations. What good would those expectations be if you just told everyone about them, but didn't hold them accountable? They would see you as an inconsistent leader who can't follow through. They would see you as someone who doesn't really value those expectations and standards like you said you did. You, as the company officer, must model the behavior you want others to emulate. If you don't hold yourself accountable to the same standards you hold your crew to, there will be resentment. Now there will be times when accountability tilts more towards the discipline side of the house and that is ok. It is important that your firefighters know that you are going to deal with problems. It is important for them to see that if someone speaks rudely to a patient, is apathetic in their duties, or does anything to degrade the integrity of the team, it will be dealt with. Have you ever been in a firehouse and seen problems occurring that are going unchecked or without interruption? What does that do to the team dynamic? What I think it does is make others who see these problems question your ability to be the boss. Often big problems got that way because they were not dealt with when they were small problems. If your crew continually sees that you choose not to hold someone accountable, it can easily create the "well, the captain doesn't care so why should I" mentality. They will grow frustrated with your inability to stop a behavior, have the difficult conversations, and work towards solutions. I know of a fire officer who was always described as an officer who "looks out for his guys." I am sure deep down this officer cared for their folks, in fact I would almost guarantee it, but where's the accountability? This same officer did little to nothing to prepare and train his firefighters. Occasionally, people would want to go work for this officer because he essentially let them do whatever the hell they wanted. There was no structure, no training, no standards. In fact, I heard a firefighter say to me one day "It's really easy to work for him. He really looks out for us. He cooks for us all the time, and really doesn't make us do a whole lot other than just run calls. That's all we have to worry about." Is looking out for your guys important? Absolutely it is, but truly look out for them. A certain amount of accountability has to exist for this to occur. Looking out for them doesn't mean covering for them, sweeping things under the rug, or doing their jobs for them. Looking out for your crews means putting their needs before yours, but not being afraid to hold them accountable to the standards, expectations, and core values of your team or organization. Looking out for your people means keeping them mission focused and prepared to get the job done. I always tell my crew that I will back them up 100% if they are right, but I will hold them 100% accountable if they are wrong. That is accountability. That is looking out for your crew.

COMMUNICATION

Open lines of communication in your firehouse are essential to the health of the team. I believe open lines of communication need to be encouraged and welcomed at all times. Communication comes in a variety of ways so let's talk about some specific examples, with the first one being, keep your people informed. There will be a lot of information that will be passed your way via supervisors and other mediums. Share that information with your crew. Keep them informed on what is going on around the department. This will do a couple things. One, it will eliminate the excuse of, "well I never heard about that" and the other thing it could sometimes do is dispel the good ole firehouse rumor mill. Your firefighters need to know that they can come to you for help with anything.

I love a quote from Colin Powell, "The day your soldiers stop bringing you their problems is the day you stopped leading them. They have either lost confidence that you can help them or concluded that you do not care. Either case is a failure of leadership." If you are going to tell people you have an open door policy, that doesn't come with exceptions. You need to create an environment where communication is welcomed and encouraged at all times. This isn't a part-time process or position you are in. I am a firm believer in the necessity of having difficult conversations and the need to openly discuss problems as well as potential solutions. If your crew feels like they can't talk to you or their fellow firefighters then problems will not be addressed, and issues will begin to fester. Many problems we face in the firehouse could have been dealt with by just having open lines of communication. I can remember on more than one occasion hearing an issue floating around the station and no one wanted to be the first to bring it up, no one wanted to say anything in hopes that it would just go away. Things just don't go away. In all of those circumstances I called everyone into a room for what people would sometimes describe as a "come to Jesus" meeting. I used that as an opportunity to address the issue with everyone in an open discussion to achieve resolution. Now, a time or two these discussions got pretty heated and emotional, but in almost all cases, there was a resolution. There was closure of an issue and it reinforced to the team that this is ok; we can talk about and fix things as a crew.

Here is the last part: listening. Yes, listening is a part of this whole communication thing and to be honest it is one of my weaknesses I am trying to get better at. I think in general most company officers are poor listeners. That may be an extreme assumption, but I am also speaking about myself. I have to make sure that when someone walks into my office, they pull me aside on a call, or just need to bend my ear and vent that I give them my full attention. This means pushing your chair away from the desk, putting away the phone, and shutting off the TV. Actually listen and pay attention to what they have to say. Don't interrupt them and offer solutions or advice midsentence. Wait until they finish what they are trying to tell you. Ask clarifying questions. How are you supposed to find a practical solution to a problem if you don't understand what they are trying to tell you? Now, not everyone comes to your office or pulls you aside looking for answers and solutions. Sometimes they just need you to listen to them. I know I know; you can picture the scene now. You invite them in, have them sit on the comfortable leather couch and encourage them to open up about what they are feeling while you sit there and nod your head. I am not talking about the cliché counselor/counselee setup, but there will be times where your firefighters just want to talk and get stuff off their chest. Listen to them and let them download. I can remember a specific case where one of my crew members came to me to tell me about a problem he was having on the ship. He started to vent out some frustrations with policy and leadership and then the conversation took a turn to his family and problems at home. He opened up to me about divorce and depression. Had I stopped at the "work related stuff" and kept offering solutions, he may have shut down. He may have thought, *"Hey idiot, I want to get help and get this stuff off my chest."* Thankfully that day, I just simply did one thing, I listened. I paid attention to what he was trying to tell me and at the end I was able to do what I could to help this person out.

Make sure you communicate with your people. Engage them, listen to them, share ideas and opinions with them, and encourage them to do the same. The team you want to build or be a part of is one that is connected to each other through conduits of trust and communication. They share and explore ideas, they talk and listen to each other, and they are not afraid to have the difficult, uncomfortable conversations. There is another word for the term uncomfortable when it comes to teams, that word is growth. You must be able to have those difficult conversations and welcome conflict; it's going to happen. The worst thing you could do is ignore that conflict thinking it will just work out. That never happens and will drive your team even further apart. More on this topic later.

SENSE OF PURPOSE

"We will the best damn engine company in the city!" This is what I told my crew on my first day. Pretty tall order, right? I think so too, and that's ok. Another part of this team building process is a sense of purpose. Often this sense of purpose comes from what's important to you. It stems from your values and beliefs and if it's not important to you, it will not be important to them. I think it's very important that you communicate to your crew as early as possible where you want to take them. By doing this it will provide them with a road map. I told my crew that we will be the ones the chief wants to see turn the corner at an incident, not because we are golfing buddies, but because he/she knows that we can be counted on. I believe by telling them this it eliminates a lot of questions or wonder about why things are flowing the way they are in the station. *Why are we doing a lot of training lately?* We will be the best damn engine in the city. *Why is the Captain worried about this?* We will be the best damn engine in the city. From my experience some firefighters just show up lost with no guidance or direction from their leadership. There is no reinforcement that the job they do is an important one and a valuable one. Take every chance you get to let your firefighters know just how important this career in service is. Show them that the job they perform everyday matters and that we have to always be ready to perform at a high level. The public is counting on us. Having and sharing a sense of purpose with your crew will be the difference between a cohesive team and one that just shows up in the same shirts and are a bunch of co-workers. It will help them achieve satisfaction in the things they do every day and make your team that much stronger. Be contagiously enthusiastic about your sense of purpose and communicate it to your crew as often as you can.

APPRECIATION

Lastly, we get to appreciation. Usually firefighters step back when they know some appreciation is headed their way, especially in the way of formal recognition. Most, if not all people, appreciate recognition when it is earned and deserved. We are all human beings and regardless of what you may say, it feels good to know that someone noticed something you did and wants to pat you on the back for it. An old fashioned "good job" is always very nice but take it a step further occasionally. I hear all the time *"I wish our chiefs would do this"* or, *"I wish our department would do that"* when it comes to different types of recognition or appreciation. This book is directed to people at the company level, the folks who normally aren't the grand decision makers when making change on the way people are recognized, at least not department wide. So, let's talk about some examples of what we can do in the firehouse. When I was a Lieutenant my crew always met in the galley after dinner for some coffee and fellowship. The driver of the Rescue Company took the lead as the barista (he might body slam me if I actually called him that). Right after dinner he would head right to the coffee pot, grind the beans, and make a nice fresh pot of coffee. He would grab everyone's mug and made their coffee just how they liked it. This was about 12 cups of coffee per night. He knew how everyone liked their coffee and passed them around when he was all done, always making his last. We would sit around the galley, drinking our coffee, telling lies and making fun of each other and just have a good time as a crew. This barista (sorry) had a favorite coffee. If I was in the store and saw a bag of this coffee, I would grab a bag for him. I would bring it to the station and he would be stoked and would give me a nice solid pound a man hug. Is there anything special about that coffee? It's just a bag of coffee, right? It was more to him, and more to that crew. It was something he appreciated, and it is something that we did together as a crew.

Another time we had a couple of probationary firefighters get off probation and we had a picture of the station made with some mat near the frame. We all signed it and gave a piece of advice, a few kind words, or a couple smartass remarks. After the famous rookie dinner, we enjoyed some cake, that awesome coffee I told you about, and then we presented the rookies with their nice picture and went around the room to have everyone say a few words. Another time we had a plaque made to give a job well done. These are just a couple of small things that are in your immediate control. One last thing I do is when someone checks into my station, they get a patch and a coin from the firehouse. Again, nothing crazy here, just a patch and a coin. By doing this it already gets the right message started. We want you as part of the team, we appreciate you, and you are a part of something here.

None of the things I have mentioned are crazy expensive. None of them need a line item in the budget and none of them require permission. There are many ways to show appreciation in your firehouse, you just need to care enough to make it happen.

I have found myself on more than one occasion saying, *"Just do this for me, please just do it for me."* What am I asking them to do here? I am asking them to dig down into that well of equity that I have hopefully built up with them. If I haven't given them a sense of purpose, built up a foundation of trust and truly appreciated them, then that well may be running dry. If I haven't done anything for them why should they return the favor? They don't have to, and sometimes they won't. They may do it because they have to, and not because they want to. When you get your team to do things because they want to and it aligns with the standards and expectations that you have set, that is a win my friends. So, build those teams. Know there will be some growing pains and that is ok. Allow the team to get better for going through it. Show them you care and appreciate them. Be honest and open in your commination, hold them accountable when they are wrong and be there for them when they are right. Give them a true sense of purpose that they are happy about. Do all of this on a bedrock of trust and you will be headed in the right direction. You may not get the results you want immediately, but be patient and persistent, those results are coming.

CHAPTER 6
TRAIN THEM

"We do not rise to the level of our expectations. We fall back to our level of training."
  -Archilochus

If you take a look at the job description of most company officers in any given fire department, I can assure you there is some mention of training. If there isn't, shame on whoever wrote that description. To give you a specific example, in my department one of the essential functions in the job description for a Lieutenant reads: Develops personnel by overseeing training operations, developing training objectives, evaluating and counseling subordinates. Pretty simple right? Well sadly, there are some who completely miss this.

I believe that training is one of the most important responsibilities you have, or will have, as a company officer. What is more important than making sure your crew members get what they need to remain ready, competent, and able? It's definitely at the top of my list. I have spent time in busy stations and time in slower stations and there is one common denominator when it comes down to performance: training. It all comes down to what that crew is doing to prepare for the next run. I have seen busy companies show up and look like circus clowns, and slower companies show up and look beautifully orchestrated in their execution, and vice versa. It all goes back to what is the priority for that crew. I can walk into a firehouse today where there are firefighters who can quote the sick leave policy and not miss a beat. They can walk that line of abuse, but they can't swing the axe and set the halligan. I have seen firefighters who can navigate the grievance procedure like a fresh lawyer out of Harvard, but they can't navigate their sorry asses down a hallway to do an effective search. That is a crew and an officer who has its priorities all screwed up.

If we conduct training the right way it can lead to efficiency, cohesion, less whining, and ultimately lives and property saved. It must start with the officer. There are certainly those places out there where an absent company officer happens to just be a seat filler and neglects the professional development of the crew. I have seen it and I'm sure you have as well. Fortunately, in some of those places there are firefighters who step up to the plate and take care of each other. Someone has to do it and if you are an officer reading this it better start with you. As the saying goes, above all else, lead by example. So, how can we make training fun, interesting, relevant, accepted, and part of the station culture? My answer would be to mix it up and take your crew motivation levels and experience into consideration. Allow me to elaborate and give some details.

When I reported to a ladder company as a Lieutenant I had a pretty young crew for the most part. The station was full of some high energy folks who could be described as self-starters with an average tenure of probably 8-10 years on the job. I knew I could work well with that energy level and leverage that enthusiasm. I had a structured training routine, especially when I first got there. I wanted to push them, see their strengths and weaknesses, take the opportunity to get to work well with them, build that trust, and reinforce my expectations. There was a lot to offer in this particular station with tech recuse, a ladder, an engine, and a medic unit. We trained quite a bit and from what I saw it was always very positive. Now, I go to a new station as a Captain and I have a crew with double the average tenure, more experience, mostly all in the latter part of their careers. Could I take the same approach with them as I could the previous crew? I could, but my results would not have been what I wanted. To be more specific, let's talk about the quantity of training from one crew to the next. I told you that when I was a Lieutenant we trained just about every day. As a Captain with a more seasoned crew, I couldn't do that every day. I know what some may be thinking, every day is a training day right? I have to be honest with you, my answer is: it depends on your crew. We talked about sizing your folks up earlier.

As a Captain with a senior crew I had to find a way to show them that this young officer full of piss and vinegar had something to offer. I had to prove to them I was able to add value to that team. I had several different levels of motivation within that group. Some very low, some higher. I needed to find a way in. I needed to figure out a way to build their motivation while not shutting them down. I couldn't use the same approach to training as my previous crew, I would have lost them. I would have shut some of them down and that is the opposite of what I was trying to achieve. I have had to learn a hard lesson and that is, not everyone thinks like me. Not everyone will think like you either. I love this job as much as the next guy and I am the type of guy who will train all day every day, if I have the crew that reciprocates. I am also the guy who knows when to turn up the heat and when to turn it down. So, this station where I was a Captain, we certainly did some training. I focused on some training topics that I felt would be interesting and practical. I also had them pick the topics they wanted to cover and invested time into setting up some quality training to cover them. They were able to see my approach towards training and that my ultimate goal was to make us all better and reinforce the concept of team and mission. Do you think we started to increase the amount of training as time went on? We sure did, but only after I was able to build relationships, trust, and harness those individual levels of motivation. I was able to do so after I got buy in from the previous training experiences they had. Once I did that these firefighters started asking for more. Because I believed in them, I believed in us as a team, and I tried to show them the value of training and what it does to build cohesion and efficiency. I would say the training tempo that I had with the high energy self-starters is exactly the same as where I got with some more seasoned senior firefighters, I just had to give a damn about my people and know I could inspire them to be better today than they were yesterday. I tried my best and they did too. I was proud of the team we were able to create.

    I mentioned that you must mix it up when it comes to training. I am a believer that this is what will help break up the routine and keep people engaged and motivated. If you took a look at my training calendar you would see a variety of topics. One day we might be in full gear stretching lines, another we may be doing pump operations. The next week we will be at the galley table talking strategy and tactics and covering SOP's. On our way to the grocery store we will stop to take a look at an FDC and talk high rise for a while. There may be some impromptu conversations about building construction as we drive to the store, then it's back in our turnout gear for some search and rescue. You must maintain a good blend of relevant training. Another thing to consider is the environment that you create when doing this training. Is it a positive one where people are encouraged to ask questions and challenge each other? Or, have you had the unfortunate experience of listening to some condescending jerk talk down to you? I have had that crummy experience myself. One of the first questions I ask myself when someone is disengaged in training, apathetic, or seems like they have something better to do is…Why do they have this attitude? Poor training experience in the past? Had that condescending officer for several years? There could be a number of reasons, but I want to get down to the root of that problem and fix it. The last thing about creating a healthy environment for training is simple: be positive and enthusiastic. If it is not important to you, it will not be important to them.

Think about your overall approach to training. What I mean is utilize the crawl before they walk type of mentality. You will have varying experience levels as I mentioned before, but here is a general path that I take with my crews when it comes to professional development. Training, Drilling, Reinforcement, Implementation of standards. It is a very simple approach for me and I have seen positive results from it.

Training to me is simply that, training. A more methodical approach to increasing the understanding of why we perform that skill and confident execution of that skill. During training I don't want people to demonstrate failure. I don't want them failing in training, they can fail later and we will get there. For me, when we conduct training it has a different tempo. There is demonstration, conversation, and detailed explanation on what I expect to see when it comes to a specific skill. Let's take deploying high rise hose for example. I would discuss the way we deploy hoe and why, I would demonstrate how to properly deploy the hose and the crew members would follow. During this time, I would stop to interject, give advice, make corrections, and allow them to try again until they felt comfortable and I was pleased with their performance. Once I saw during training that they grasped the concepts, it was onto the drill.

Drilling is now a time to see them perform the skills they learned during training. With little to no interruption from you, the company officer, the instructor. Sticking with high-rise hose deployments, now would be their opportunity to come off the truck, report to a specific floor and deploy the hose just like they learned in training. Drilling is an opportunity for me to see if they retained anything and even more importantly can execute the skills at an acceptable level. Here you can even add stressors into your drill to make it more realistic. I would allow them to finish the evolution and once finished we would go back and critique what happened. Only here would I speak up. Here is where I am ok if they demonstrate failure. They will have an opportunity to fix it with reinforcement of those skills. Simply put, I don't like to take people out and say ok go, perform this skill I want to see how you guys do, without providing adequate training beforehand. It's not fair to them.

After we have trained and drilled, now it's time to see what's working and what isn't. Is more remediation needed? Do we need to provide further training before we can drill again? Was something missed or do I need to take a different approach to how we trained on the skill?

With reinforcement might come repetition and possibly even sitting down with someone to see why there are deficiencies. The bottom line is, there are corrections that need to be made and drilling allowed you to identify some shortfalls. Fix them and get back on track. We can go way down the rabbit hole on how to correct deficiencies, but just ensure you use the appropriate resources and focus on the problem.

If after all of this training, drilling, and reinforcement I am satisfied with performance, we create a standard. Now depending on your agency, you may have several standards to your operations. Some places have none. How long will it take to get a line on the ground, water to the nozzle and masked up? What's your standard? How about deploying 200ft of high-rise hose on the 10th floor? When it comes to my standards, I am looking for time as well as performance. If a specific skill was performed in a timely manner, but there were errors along the way, that doesn't cut it. I am looking for a combination of both. After all, when we show up, the public demands professionalism and so should we.

There have been plenty of times when I have purposely pushed my crew, and times where I have asked myself if I have pushed a little too hard. I always go back to the quote by General Bruce Clark that you saw earlier: "You owe it to your men to require standards which are for their benefit even though they may not be popular at the time." I know when I was a firefighter I didn't appreciate just how hard on *Me* my Captain was until he was no longer my Captain, and I appreciated it even more so when I became a Company Officer. I owe a lot to that man. The final piece that I would offer is this, be careful about the downtime you give them. You have heard me say numerous times already that we have to stay mission focused. That means every single day. You also need to meet the needs of your crew as I described. Downtime is a good thing, and it's important, but the mission comes first every time. Don't tilt so far over towards the needs of the crew where simply the harmony of the station and their satisfaction is what takes priority. Good officers need to know how to find balance and tip the scales appropriately. Often time's preparation and accomplishment of the mission builds confident firefighters and confident firefighters are happy firefighters.

In closing, let's talk about your training as a Company Officer. A Company Officer, to me, is an instructor. With that comes the obligation for you to constantly seek improvement. First off, if no time was spent being a good firefighter, then likely there will be struggle as an officer. I mean really, how are you supposed to teach and develop other firefighters if you haven't done that same for yourself? People will see right through that and you will lack credibility. You must ensure you take time to keep up with your professional development. Attend seminars on leadership and management. Take hands-on classes focused on basic fire ground fundamentals, improve your EMS skills in simulation labs, and more. If you want to maintain a constant cycle of producers within your organization, develop yourself first, and then others around you. If we do not do this, people will fall into the role of a company officer who have never had any good foundation of training to supplement their experience. They will stumble upon a promotion because they can navigate an assessment center only to fail in the development of their crew. How are they going to teach others when no one taught them, or they didn't take any individual responsibility to make it happen? The mad cycle will continue. Remember that you are a walking, talking, living, breathing officer development program and the example you set and the actions you take are being watched by your crew every single day you are in that uniform. Formal officer development programs are great, but that isn't a process, it's a product. Invest time in the process of the development of others long-term. Don't let them down. Prepare them, motivate and inspire them, train them right, and train them often. That is the cycle we want to maintain. That is the cycle that breeds a healthy organization full of people who produce. It's all about training!

CHAPTER 7
YOU HAVE ALL THE POWER YOU NEED

"Real power has to do with one's ability to influence the hearts and minds of others."
-Dali Lama

THIS CHAPTER WILL SERVE AS a brief, albeit important reminder about your stance as a company officer and your ability to have positive influence. Before I began my first operational assignment as a company officer, I spent some time in the training division. Right before I came out, I was talking to a very senior captain who I have a lot of respect for. I was telling him about my assignment and how I was looking forward to going back out to the station and having a crew to work with. I went on and on about how I was excited and he kind of stopped me in my tracks as I was talking. He said to me, "Yeah that's great, but just so you know, the company officers don't have any power out here anymore. Everything is in the hands of the Battalion Chief and you really can't do anything with your crews anymore because of all this oversight." What he said kind of deflated me a little bit. I understood he was trying to tell me, but I knew that I needed to form my own opinions once I got out to the street. It wasn't long after I reported to my firehouse that I quickly realized what that captain said wasn't true at all. In fact, I had total control over what I wanted to accomplish. I just had to put forth the effort, lead by example, and earn their trust; all important ingredients that we discussed in previous chapters to build a successful team.

My job as a company officer is to teach my firefighters how to be good at their job and also mentor them to take my position if they ever choose to at some point in their career. As far as I'm concerned too many people spend time worrying about things that are completely out of their control. I think if company officers and firefighters focused on things that they had immediate control over our departments and our firehouses would improve overnight. I am talking about things like forcing doors, stretching lines, ground ladders, performing good searching rescue, top notch EMS care, and any other responsibilities that you may have at the company level. Not only do you have an immediate control over those things, you also have control over the actions and behavior of every single one of your crewmembers. Assuming you've laid out a set of standards and expectations, you can hold them accountable to those expectations. I'm sure everybody has heard something called the sphere of influence or sphere of concern. I can remember a Battalion Chief giving me some advice one day after receiving the news about a transfer. He told me it doesn't matter where you end up; you make it yours. He said if you go to station 2 you make station 2 the best damn station in the city. If you go to station 13 you better do the same damn thing there. He was essentially telling me to worry about my fishbowl and focus on the things I had immediate control over. He also went on to say that I should not waste my time on things outside my firehouse. I should not grow frustrated with things that other firefighters or other company officers do. Why? Because they are not in my fishbowl. They are not the ones I can reach out and touch and have immediate control over. Come to find out this it is extremely difficult to sit back and watch at times, but I quickly turn my head towards my crew and focus on making sure they are better and would never do the things that I see feeding my frustrations. I remain focused on them and their professional development and well-being.

I briefly mentioned it in a previous chapter, but I want to elaborate on an experience I had at my station as a new captain. I mentioned that one thing you should never do as a new officer going to any station is prejudge your crew. This is one of the biggest mistakes you can make. You should form your own opinions and make your decisions based off the foundation of trust you have built with them and not the opinions of others. My experience there was a classic example of how I had all the power that I needed to make immediate change within that station. I briefly mentioned in Chapter 2 what people were filling my head with before I reported. Essentially, they were telling me I was going to run into all kinds of problems there. Like any new station assignment there was going to be those growing pains. Were there problems there? Yes, but not problems that couldn't be fixed. One of the first things I did when arriving at this station as the captain was try to build relationships. I wanted the crew to know that while I was the captain, my job here was to add value to the team and that's exactly what I told them the first morning in that galley at line-up. I simply want to add value to the team. My job was to show them they can add value to the team as well, just as long as they put forth an effort. You are going to have all sorts of ideas on how you want to run the firehouse, things you may want to accomplish and maybe even some changes that you want to make. It will be extremely difficult if you don't take the time to build relationships. For the first few weeks at firehouse I really sat back and observed the actions and behaviors of these firefighters. I watched how they interacted with each other, as well as me, as their new officer. Once I felt comfortable I was earning some trust, I wanted to show them how I can add value to the team and make them better firefighters today than they were the day before. This is when I started to conduct a consistent training program, as well as interrupt some actions and behaviors that may have been allowed to take place previously, but did not meet my standards and expectations. During these training sessions I worked hard to make them relevant and show them the positive outcome that could result from their hard work. When it came to interrupting behavior, I corrected things quickly and firmly when I saw they went against the values I wanted to see in them as firefighters. Weeks would go by and I would have conversation after conversation about problems that were allowed to fester for too long. For the most part I had success in those conversations because I was always able to tie them back to the standards and expectations that were laid out when I first reported. There were no surprises for them. They knew the principles on which all my decisions were made. Everything would be done in their best interest, the interest of the station, and the department. I can remember thinking to myself at one point that I was not going to make any progress in certain areas, and these guys want nothing to do with what I want to accomplish over here, but I didn't give up. I stayed true to those principles, values, and what I expect of others around me. There were times, quite frankly, when I couldn't wait to find myself on the next transfer list. I had to remain positive and focus on the development of that team. I know for a fact that they had their doubts about me as well and that's ok. In the end it all works out if we understand we have all the power we need right at the tips of our fingers to influence and win people over. It is not through policy or general orders. It is not done by finger pointing and yelling. It is done through a clear sense of purpose, expectations, and some accountability. Oh yeah, and you better be leading by example also. Did I have authority over them as a captain to do all these things? Sure, I did, but I don't want to act on authority alone. People will certainly follow you because they have to, but its better when they follow you because they want to. When they have to, they hesitate, they become apprehensive. When they want to follow you that is where true leadership, followership, and teamwork will thrive. After the first few months we started to get in a groove at the station. They were starting to grow comfortable with me and I was starting to grow comfortable with them. We started to have that sense of unity and cohesion within the firehouse that everyone told me I was not going to be able to achieve. I even remember people telling me I wasn't changing anyone over there and it's a waste of time to try. That I should just show up and work on myself and focus on something else for a while. I had people tell me the crew and I were going to have a rough relationship the whole time and that it would just be miserable. The growing pains we all went through are normal and necessary for the growth of any team. If we avoid that we are sure to derail every chance we have of forming a strong team. This will be discussed more in the next chapter as we talk about having those difficult conversations.

So, take it for me: you have all the power you need to influence and make positive change within your firehouse. I am extremely proud of my crew and what we were able to accomplish. For me, that's a win. Did I need my Battalion Chief's permission to do any of that? No, I did not. My Shift Commander's, my Deputy Chief's, or my Fire Chief's permission to make any of these changes within my firehouse? Absolutely not, because I had all the power I needed as a company officer to make positive change in my firehouse. Can you imagine the condition of your firehouses if we all take that much ownership of our crews? If we all sacrificed just a little bit of ourselves to make others better? Even greater, if every firehouse felt the same way, what would your fire department look like? It's not a pipedream and it can happen. It starts with you.

Let me close out this chapter by addressing another thing I see. Every now and then I see a company officer who has completely checked out. What I mean by that is they have grown so frustrated at some point in their career that they have completely neglected their duties and responsibilities as a company officer. Now I'm not saying that some great officers and firefighters can't be driven into apathy. Unfortunately, I have seen it, and the leadership that does this to good people should be ashamed of themselves. Maybe you are close to being in that position now. Maybe somewhere down the road this might be you. My advice to you would be don't look up the chain of command, look down the chain of command. Focus on your crews and what you have immediate control over. Set a good example for them despite how you think you may have been treated. Set a good example for them especially when others are not doing it for you. If you do this, if we do this, we can hold onto the hope that those folks will never have to experience what you did and will continue to move throughout the organization with optimism, positivity, and focus on what it takes to make people around them great. They will also understand they will have all the powers they need to make their company great if they are ever in the position to be a company officer.

CHAPTER 8
THE NOT-SO-EASY CONVERSATIONS

"Speak the truth even if your voice shakes when you do it."

-Maggie Kuhn

There are going to be some times during your journey as a company officer that are not always going to be pleasant. There are going to be times you must make sure you don't let your emotions get the best of you. There will be times when you must have difficult conversations if you want to ensure the success of individuals and the team as a whole. We are going to spend some time this chapter talking about how to manage some conflict that may arise in your firehouse, how to make those difficult conversations a little bit easier to handle, and a process that I use when it comes to dealing with problems in my firehouse.

In my opinion the main reason we don't approach difficult conversations, or maybe the reason we refuse to have them altogether, is because they tend to have an emotional reaction. What I mean by that is, if you were to sit somebody down in your office today or maybe at the galley table for a cup of coffee and explain something to them that was becoming a problem, you may get some type of emotional response or even outburst. I have experienced somebody becoming completely angry and yelling at me after I tried to address a problem. Now comes the aftermath, right? Will it create tension at the station? Will it make things awkward? We have a station outing planned and this is going to make things weird. It doesn't matter. These conversations must take place. Likely what's driving the reason for the having the difficult conversation is the topic. Some things are just easier to address than others. Talking to someone about a missing report vs. a bad attitude are two totally different topics, but I bet one of these is easier than the other for you. We are human beings and, for the most part, we tend to naturally avoid conflict altogether. None of us come to work looking forward to having difficult conversations and challenging others to the point where it will drive an emotional response out of somebody, especially anger. It's because of these emotional responses, I think as supervisors, it's easier to just avoid the problem altogether. I have even rationalized in my own mind once or twice, "If I just let it go, the problem will go away and it won't resurface." That is the wrong way to handle things. Things never just fix themselves, and most times big problems started off as small problems. If only we had addressed the problem when it was small, we might not be in the predicament we are in today. You have an obligation as the company officer to have those difficult conversations. So, here's the rest of my advice on how to best have those and solve some problems in your firehouse.

We have talked a little bit about how to build relationships with people in your firehouse, and I will tell you there are always two sides to any conflict that you may have to manage. The first is the issue, or whatever problem you're trying to deal with. The second part is the relationship that you have with that person. In my experience I have found that if I take the time to work on building a relationship with somebody, the less time it takes to sit down and have a difficult conversation with them before we reach successful outcomes. That hasn't worked every time, but the majority of difficult conversations I had to have with people were successful because I took the time to get to know the person first. You have to remember to separate the issue from the person, and deal with the issue. Growing that relationship with the individual allows you to do that. They will understand that the conversation is about the issue at hand. Now there are going to be times where you may not have a chance to build that relationship. I have been in situations before where I haven't had much time with the crew and I immediately have to address behavior or actions that are taking place. I haven't had time to build those relationships, but I have to confront the issue immediately anyway. Your approach to this issue will determine your success. When you're sitting down with this person, ask yourself, "How do I minimize the chance of conflict?" Another question I find myself asking is, "Why? Why has this issue come up? Why does this person act or feel this way?" It is your job to uncover the root causes of some of the behavior you will see. If somebody has a bad attitude, I want to know why they have a bad attitude. If somebody is apathetic towards training, I want to know why they feel that way. Was is it a previous officer who maybe used training as a punishment? Was a previous officer, who didn't handle problems well and didn't confront problems, leading to this person having a bad attitude?" There could be a whole host of reasons but there's always a root cause of everything and we need to try to figure out what that is. Many times, the behaviors you see for the attitudes you have to confront are merely symptoms. As a company officer you have to treat the disease. The first thing you must do is be in control of your emotions. The biggest mistake you can make as a supervisor is act off emotions such as anger or frustration and not off of logic. If you need to wait a day or two to address the problem, especially if time will allow, then do so. What you say today out of anger might be something you will regret tomorrow when you have a clear head.

    I'm going to cover a process I use to handle a lot of the problems that arise in my firehouse. It's not a flawless system but has been proven to help with the majority of the difficult conversations I've had. This process cannot solve every single problem in your firehouse. If it does that is great, but you need to form your own process based off the specific individuals you are responsible for. Remember how I talked about sizing people up in an earlier chapter? Knowing your people will allow you to adjust. This process is a blend of some things I've learned along the way in both the military, the fire service and even watching other presentations. One in particular was a presentation from Myron Radio of the R group. The R group is a group of professionals that help teams through organizational change and transition. I have tweaked a few things here and there, and this was the final result. It may be similar to other workplace conflict management techniques whether in corporate America or your downtown firehouse. Feel free to alter this process even further or just cherry pick what you like and discard what you don't. While the process may be similar to dozens of others I have seen, it is the content of the conversation, your body language, and your overall approach that will be the contributing factors to your success. Before we cover this process in detail, the first thing I want you to do is view obstacles as opportunity. If we start off by immediately thinking that these obstacles are going to be nothing but a pain in the butt, cause more work for us, and be a complete frustrating ordeal then we are starting off on the wrong foot and we make the option of simply ignoring the option of ignoring the issue easier. We must view these obstacles as opportunity. Not just an opportunity to fix the problem, but an opportunity for growth for both you as a supervisor or company officer, and for the other person across the table from you. If handled well these difficult conversations can turn out very positive in the end. If handled well these conversations will help to grow the relationship between you and the person you are working with.

I think you know how much I care about developing people. Let's say this person that you are having a conversation with decides to be a company officer one-day. Now it's their turn to have a difficult conversation with somebody. I can bet he/she will remember the tone and emotion of the conversation you had with them at one point and he/she will use that to help with having the difficult conversations in his fire house, creating a positive domino effect. If we all get to a place where this happens, where there is smart accountability across the board and people meet challenges head-on, imagine what your department would look like.

Now that we're in the right mindset let's outline this process. It is a five-step process that includes the following:

1. Address the problem.
2. Why are we here?
3. What are we going to do about this?
4. What can I do to help you?
5. Follow-up and provide support.

ADDRESS THE PROBLEM

Addressing the problems can be one of the very first things you do. When you do this, you need to be very direct in your delivery. Be very specific about the issue you want to address. If you remain too vague you will steer off track. Let's use an apathetic approach towards training to move through this process. You can certainly plug your issue or any issue into this, but we will use this as I have seen and heard from many people across the country that this is not an uncommon challenge in a firehouse. If I were very vague, I may say something like, "You know, Jarrod, you have a really bad attitude towards training." This person will likely shut down as soon as they hear you tell them that they have a bad attitude. To them, this may be a character assassination. There's a better way to put it even if you still feel like they have a bad attitude. I told you to be specific so try something like this: "Jarrod, the problem is last Wednesday the crew was out training and I noticed you didn't want to get involved in stretching hose lines on the side of the station. I watched everybody work while you stood off to the side and didn't put your hands on the hose and didn't really offer up any conversation to the team. You seemed very withdrawn and it concerned me." Now you have given a very specific example of the problem you want to address. Give as much detail about the incident as possible.

WHY ARE WE HERE?

This next step is a for you to explain why this conversation is so important to you. You really want to drive home the point that this topic is an important one and deserves some attention for a very specific reason. Sticking with the training problem you might say something like this: "Jarrod, the reason we are here having this conversation is because training is very important to me and the performance of our station as a whole. I believe we have a responsibility to be good at our jobs and when I see a member of the team looking disconnected it concerns me and I want to fix it." Once again, you're very direct here. Whatever the problem is you need to explain to them why it is important to you that you two are in this room talking about this problem and having this conversation. If needed you can add things like policy and core values. Specifically values that you have set for the team. Remember values are just words if there's no accountability piece to give them meaning. At the end of the second step you really want them to understand why this problem is important to you and why it should be important to them too.

WHAT ARE WE GOING TO DO ABOUT THIS?

What are we going to do about it? This is the question that you're going to pose to them to fix the problem.

Remember to be brief and keep the conversation focused on the issue. The reason I like to ask them this question is because it puts the accountability on them. It transfers ownership of the problem to their side of the table. After you ask them this question you need to be quiet and listen to what they have to say. You may end up getting some excuses but always go back to the question, "What are we going to do about it?" Now there are certainly some solutions that you have in your mind. For this training example I'm sure you want this person to become more engaged, to be actively involved, and to offer input in future training sessions. As they offer some of their own solutions to fix the problem you can repeat the question as needed to drive them to your solutions as well, and in the end without that person even realizing it they met you halfway and now you have both landed on a realistic solution. When I say repeat the question, you would repeat it after they offer a solution. It may sound something like this: Jarrod might say to you, "Well captain I guess the next time we do training I'll make it a point to step into the rotation and actually put my hands on some hose and stretch some lines." As Jarrod's supervisor you would say "That sounds great, what else are we going to do about it?" You would continue to ask that follow-up question to allow them to provide more solutions. Don't force it on them, but repeat as needed until they have thought of all they could do to solve the problem. Again, this allows them to provide their own solutions in parallel with yours. What it also does is force the ownership on them. So later, if this conversation were to arise again you can hold them accountable to the solutions they set for themselves. What I want to avoid as their supervisor is coming back to them in a few months or whatever timeline you have set and say "remember when I told you…" Now you can approach them when following up and say "remember when *you* told me…" This is their issue to fix. You are there to provide support and guidance, but they own it. The hardest part about this step is actively listening to somebody. Turn off the computer, turn off your TV, put your phone in your drawer and spend time actively listening to the person across the table or across the room from you. It's important for them to know they have your undivided attention.

WHAT CAN I DO TO HELP YOU?

This question only comes in the end. At this point, hopefully, they have come up with some solutions and the ownership has been transferred to them. Remember this issue has nothing to do with you and everything to do with them, so keep the conversation focused on the solutions. I have seen what this process can do to help in the conversations I've had with people. When I apply this process, when I ask them what I can do to help, they are genuine in their responses. I have even had people open up about some of the root causes of why they may be acting this way. I've seen people become very apologetic about the way they have been performing or behaving. Again, listen to them but keep the ownership moving in their direction. You need to be genuine as well. If you're going to ask somebody what you can do to help them and they tell you what they want or expect, you need to be there for them. Be prepared to offer the support and/or the resources they may need to improve their performance.

FOLLOW-UP/PROVIDE SUPPORT

This last step is very simple, but one of the easiest to forget. The first piece of advice I would give you is to document the conversation in its entirety. You may not need that documentation at all, but if problems continue to fester and don't have any resolution you may have refer to this documentation for further correction in the future. If possible, figure out a way to set up a follow-up conversation. There are a variety of ways to do this. Put a reminder in your phone or maybe even in your work calendar at the firehouse. Is very easy to get sidetracked, especially after a productive conversation. Don't fall into the trap that simply because you had a good conversation, and you're able to identify some solutions, that you just don't have to revisit it. Take the time to follow up with that person and see what they need, see how they're doing, and see if there is any additional support you may have to provide. This follow-up conversation doesn't have to be anything formal. It can simply be a tailboard or front bumper conversation with a hot cup of coffee and some honest dialogue.

Like anything else, well laid plans can completely derail and I have seen it happen. I have moved through this process and met resistance. The conversation explodes and does not go the way you want it to and you need to take a break. The first person in that room to lose control of their emotions, loses. Once that has happened you can no longer have a productive conversation and need to walk away. This has happened to me a couple times and I have had tell the person across from me that I don't want to have an argument, I want to have a conversation and the point we are at right now we cannot have a productive conversation. Consider having the conversation somewhere else. Sometimes simply moving out of the office and maybe into the apparatus bay or outside at a park bench relaxes the shoulders a little bit. You'll have to apply policy as necessary, especially if the problem is very specific to that policy.

Lastly, involve your supervisors. I'm a company officer and for the other company officers that are reading this we answer to a chief officer. Not everything you are going to run across can be dealt with at your level, so involve your chiefs as necessary and lean on them for support.

Something I will also leave you with in this chapter is picking your battles. I have had people tell me there is no such thing as picking battles and you should pick every single one. Basically, what they were saying is if there is an infraction of any kind, whether it goes against policy or otherwise, it must be addressed. That you must pick every battle, so you remain consistent. I am not saying this person is wrong, that is just not my style. Quite frankly I always pick my battles. I think there are times when we can't be so black and white with things and need to see in shades of gray.

The first thing you must understand is the scope of your authority. For example, if you get in a heated conversation with an employee and tell them "I am going to have your job for this" that is beyond your scope of authority. I have heard stories of company officers saying this to someone. That is a very extreme example, but stick to what's in your control. Before you choose to pick any battle, you must have a solution in mind. You can tie this back to that sense of purpose or values we talked about. Is the issue you are considering addressing going against those values or getting in the way of that sense of purpose? If so, it may be worth going after and a battle you are willing to fight. I ask my crew members all the time when they are considering putting up a fight on a certain issue "Is this the hill you want to die on? If so, then charge on." I would ask you the same about the issue you may have to deal with. For me a general rule on whether or not I will pick a battle comes down to what it will have an impact on if not addressed. If the issue could create conflict and have an impact on the station, the department, the city or the public, then I will pick that battle. If that issue interferes with my expectations and values at the firehouse then I will pick that battle.

I am also willing to let things go here and there. You've seen the cop shows where the smooth detective says he/

she is willing to let the small fish go to get the big fish? I am kind of in the same mindset at times. I am willing to pick my battles to accomplish something on a grander scale. Let me give you a specific example. I had a firefighter one time who I was really having a hard time reaching and developing a relationship with. I was working hard to earn his trust and was meeting a lot of resistance. While trying to build this relationship and earn his trust there were several times I had to address uniform infractions, behavioral issues, and performance. I honestly started to feel like the only conversations we shared were over problems. It got to the point where there was little conversation about anything else. I was feeling like I was making no progress. One day this firefighter came in just a few minutes late. He is not normally late to work, and this was actually the first time he was late since I was his Captain. I know he was expecting to be counseled over it because he walked in the galley at one point and said "I'm sure you want to talk to me and do some paperwork don't you?" I just replied, "No. We are all late at some point and I trust you and know you will fix it and not let it become a habit." He looked at me a bit confused and just said, "Thank you, I really appreciate that." Now, by policy should I have written him up for being late? Yes, I should have. Was I wrong by not counseling him over being late? Maybe I was, but I wanted to throw the guy a bone. I wanted to see if by extending him this olive branch and letting it go, he would see that I would find a way to wiggle through that barrier that was up and really begin to build a relationship and earn his trust. I think it helped and there was definitely a relaxation in his shoulders. Were there times after this incident where I addressed infractions? Of course, there were, and they were addressed because those things had an impact on the team building process and sense of purpose I had for that firehouse. I am willing to pick my battles. I am willing to let some things go. I will give people a break here and there if it means I will see the rewards later. I will do it to let them know that I will not crawl over everything that they do. Again, this is just my style. I don't expect anyone here reading this to do exactly what I am explaining. I share this with you because I have found picking my battles leads to balance and keeps me focused on the big fish, if you will.

Difficult conversations are just that, they are difficult, and depending on the topics involved they will surely make them even more of a challenge. It is my hope that this chapter has offered you some sort of guidance to allow you to tackle those conversations with confidence. One of the worst things you could do as a company officer is to just ignore a problem that will impact the health of the team. Consider picking some battles if necessary and remember the power of a good old-fashioned honest tailboard conversation. Sometimes we lose sight of the power of conversation.

CHAPTER 9
SOME ADMINISTRATIVE STUFF - PERFORMANCE EVALUATIONS & TIME MANAGEMENT

"Time is the scarcest resource, and unless it is managed nothing else can be managed."
-Peter Drucker

I HAVEN'T REALLY SPOKEN HEAVILY about the administrative responsibilities that come with being a company officer. I don't want to talk about report writing, grievance procedures, or anything like that. But I want to talk about two things I think are vitally important for you. The first one is performance evaluations, and the second is time management. I get it, these aren't sexy topics, but they are important to me and I want to share my thoughts and hopefully offer some help with the way you manage your time and give a performance evaluation.

Let's start with the evaluations. I can remember, when I was in the Navy, we had an evaluation every year, much like most fire departments or any organization really. One specific evaluation I had a supervisor walk up to me and tell me I needed to write my own evaluation and give it to them when I was done. I am not quite sure why this was done. I don't know if the intent was to make me a better supervisor by learning how to write evals, but it was very impersonal.

My fire department has a pretty good evaluation process in my opinion. There are specific things a firefighter will be measured against and the process itself is easy to follow and understand. Like anything else, you can have a good product, but if the end user does not apply themselves or take it seriously, you will end up with a poor result. As a company officer you need to take the evaluation process seriously. Unfortunately, many officer development programs fail to teach how to give an effective performance evaluation. They may explain the process, when they are required, and where to access the forms, but that's it.

Think of your own organizations. Are you being taught how to give an effective and honest evaluation? Not just how to fill out the documentation, but how to interact with your people and have the conversation? How about little tips that may help your evaluation process go smoothly before its even time to sit down in the office and talk to someone about their performance? If you have that now, that's great. If you don't, maybe some of this will help you and encourage you to help other people in your organization.

One of the first things you have to be is honest. You

must give honest feedback to your folks or you are doing them a dis-service. I can remember having a firefighter who worked in my station and he was having some problems in the firehouse. He not only had behavioral issues, but performance issues as well. His previous evaluation was done about 8 months prior and when reading the evaluation, he looked like a stellar firefighter. High marks, exceeded expectations in several areas, and plenty of nice things to say about his performance. I really did some head scratching and was wondered if I was looking at the same guy. Now, to be fair I let some time go by and thought, well maybe this evaluation is correct, and I just haven't seen this side of him. That side never showed up. In fact, as time went on, he was the opposite of everything that was in that eval. It begged the question, was he given an honest evaluation? Does he know the areas he needs to work on? In this case, it was clear the honesty piece was missing. In fact, when it came time to do his evaluation the chief reviewing my eval and his last eval (the dishonest one) was really confused. At one point he said to me after reading my evaluation of this firefighter "This doesn't seem right compared to his last eval. Are you sure this is accurate?" I replied, "One of two things happened here sir, either I lied on this evaluation, or the person before me did, and I always give a fair and honest evaluation." So, you can see the problems that can be created by not being honest with someone. In the end, when it came time to sit down with this firefighter and go over my evaluation of him, he was taken back, but understood everything I told him. There were no surprises and I used specific examples of why I gave him low marks. I also gave him ways to improve.

When I say there were no surprises that's because throughout the whole previous year if I saw a problem with behavior or performance, it was addressed. I didn't walk by problems. I would always pull people aside and let them know how they were doing, and even if they were doing great, I tried to tell them that also. This made it easier when it came time for the annual review. We essentially just re-visited everything we had discussed over the last year.

If you are not providing feedback to your crews throughout the year, you are wrong. You can't simply pull someone into the office once a year and explain to them in 10 minutes everything that has happened in the last 12 months and then say, "sign here, see ya next year." That is poor evaluation. The best example I can land on for someone who provides constant feedback is a coach. Coaches are consistently providing feedback to their players. They interrupt behavior or stop it completely. There is a conversation, they note the discrepancy, offer a solution and re-evaluate. There are also solutions offered by the player to allow for some individual ownership of the problem. Coaches get it right and a company officer and a coach aren't very different. Let's look at the description of a coach:

The role of a coach is not just coaching. Sports coaches assist athletes in developing to their full potential. They are responsible for training athletes in a sport by analyzing their performances, instructing in relevant skills and by providing encouragement.

Now let's replace coach with company officer, athletes with firefighters and the word sport with profession:

The role of a company officer is not just coaching. Company Officers assist firefighters in developing to their full potential. They are responsible for training firefighters in a profession by analyzing their performances, instructing in relevant skills and by providing encouragement.

Not too much of a difference is there? By consistently providing your firefighters with feedback throughout the year it will make it that much easier when it's time to sit down for the formal evaluation. Before I give someone their evaluation, I always give them a two week heads up that it is coming. That allows them to mentally prepare for the conversation. That may not seem like a big deal, but some people really stress out about their annual performance evaluation. I also ask them to take the next couple of weeks to think about things they have accomplished over the last year I should know about and may have an impact on their evaluation. I try to keep up with everything my crew is doing but someone may have gone out to take a few classes that I wasn't aware of or did something around the station that I missed. I have a folder for every one of my guys and I try to update their folder with all the little positive, and not so positive things, that happen over the year. This helps me keep track when it comes time to hop on the computer and write the evaluation.

The next thing you want to try and do is avoid the halo or the horns effect. This was advice a chief of mine gave me and I thought it was very good. What he meant was if you are working on someone's evaluation that has been a poor performer for the majority of the year, and there is a spike in their performance or maybe even genuine improvement over the last couple of weeks, they don't get the halo effect. Meaning, they get a good evaluation based off the last two weeks of good performance while you forget about the rest of the year that was lackluster. The flip side of that is a high performing firefighter that maybe hit a couple bumps in the road come evaluation time doesn't get slammed with bad marks based off the last two to three weeks. Consider the high performer they have also been throughout the year. By remembering to avoid this halo or horns effect it will make you take a broader look at their performance. My last piece of advice when it comes to giving your evaluations is to let them read the evaluation before you bring them in for the final discussion. Whenever I complete an evaluation, I print it off and give it to that firefighter. I tell them to look it over carefully and that we will discuss everything I have written. I make sure they can come to me with questions before we sit down in the office to discuss it further. For me this does one thing. If there was going to be an emotional reaction to the content, like them being pissed off about something, I want them to have that reaction before we finally sit down to go over it thoroughly. It gives them some time to process what is being said about their performance. Again, if you have been truthful with them all year and truthful in your evaluation, there shouldn't be much of a surprise. I have written an evaluation where I was sure I was going to have one angry firefighter with something I wrote. That wasn't the case, in fact he just shrugged his shoulders and said, "Yeah I guess we have talked about that more than once." I usually give them the eval a couple of days before we sit down in the office and talk. I don't want them to have a reaction, if they were going to have one at all, right when we sit down to chat. I want there to be a productive conversation. By letting them read through it, it takes the edge off, if needed. At the end of every performance evaluation I take the opportunity to revisit my expectations and I ask them two very important questions:

1. Is there anything else I could be doing to help with your performance or development?
2. As your supervisor is there anything else you think I could be doing better?

Be ready to hear some honest feedback. If you can give it, you better be ready to receive it as well. The 360-degree feedback will only make you a better company officer. I think this last step is important in the overall development of the team and also helps build that trust which we all know is so important in your firehouse. There are so many different types of evaluation processes out there, many driven by human resources. Whatever systems you have, I hope you can take away some nuggets here on how to give a good performance evaluation. Give them meaning, take them seriously, and always be honest with your firefighters.

TIME MANAGEMENT

Time is a resource that needs to be managed like anything else. I always chuckle at the leader vs manager debate. As a company officer I feel you have to be both. Some days more of one than the other, but both are important. Managing time is important especially when dealing with several members in a firehouse. You may find yourself being pulled in many different directions on any given day. You have those evaluations we just talked about, reports, last minute meetings, school inspections, apparatus displays, vehicle service, and of course, run a bunch of calls in the middle of all that. I will share with you just a few of the things that help keep my scattered brain in check as I navigate my day and manage my time.

DELEGATE RESPONSIBILITY

Sometimes you need to know when it is ok to hand something off to someone else. Maybe you have a junior officer on your shift who can share the responsibility. I'm sure many of us have capable and motivated firefighters who would gladly help out as long as we ask. This will help get things accomplished and it will help by giving them some additional responsibility. Certainly, follow up, but if you are going to delegate responsibility make sure you provide the resources and set people up for success.

KEEP A CALENDAR

I mainly use a calendar to schedule training ahead of time. This helps me keep track of what we have accomplished throughout the year. A calendar can also be helpful by allowing you to schedule other events such as inspections. It's no different than a personal calendar you keep at home. This one just keeps track of the events in your station. We have an outlook calendar that the whole shift can access to see what's going on, but the one I keep is just for my station and it seems to help me stay on track with what's going on in the firehouse.

KEEP A TO-DO LIST

I am a sticky note freak! I am constantly making little to-do lists throughout my day. I also have the memory of a fish, so this is just another helpful tool. I mainly make one in the morning that I try and stick to. I make it after I have figured out what I want to get done and after my Chief has filled me in on any additional items following the morning phone call. Once I have my list I prioritize what needs to get done. I simply triage what's on my list like I would a set of patients. I have three categories that I kick everything into. High, medium, and low priority.

High priority items are the things that have an impact on operational readiness. For example, the ladder company has a large hydraulic leak, or we are missing some hose off the engine company. These are the things that need to get accomplished before I move to anything else on my list. Next is medium priority. For something to fall in this category there has to be some sort of time constraint. Maybe the Chief needs to meet with us at 1300 right after lunch, or we have to have this training done by 1500 today. Anything that has an immediate deadline will fall into this category. Lastly, low priority. This is something with no time constraint and it doesn't have an impact on operational readiness. So, after I look at my day and triage my to-do list, I can decide on what we will do first, second, or maybe even what gets kicked down the road to another shift.

Alright, we are all done with the admin stuff. That wasn't so bad was it? This is certainly not the sexy stuff we like to think about when we think about being a company officer. But is extremely important. We talk a whole lot about being a leader in this book. Be a good manager also. Manage yours and your crew's time wisely and value the importance and impact an honest and meaningful performance evaluation can have.

CHAPTER 10
GO OUT AND MAKE THE DIFFERENCE

"I've learned that people will forget what you said, people will forget what you did, but people will never forget how you made them feel."
-Maya Angelou

Here we are at the last chapter. In the Introduction of this book I explained to you my whole goal was to offer you some substance so you can walk into your firehouses and make some positive change. I hope I was able to give you some realistic ideas you can put to good use. Maybe even some of my advice triggered some new ideas in your mind. If you want to be a good leader just get out there and lead. You're going to make mistakes, you're going to look back on decisions you made and wonder if they were right or wrong, in the end if you're acting in the best interest of the people you're responsible for, you can't go wrong. I believe all the way down to my core that the company officer plays such a vital role in the health of an organization. So many positive changes can take place right in your firehouse if you just give a damn about your people and stay committed to your responsibility. Above you can see a quote that I used from Maya Angelou. I wanted to share a story with you to close out this book. This story falls right in line with what Dr. Angelou was telling us. I'm not sharing the story with you to make myself feel better. I'm sharing this story with you to remind you that what you do out there truly matters.

When I was in the Navy, I held the role of what is called the work center supervisor. I had about five or six sailors who worked for me and we were responsible for many of the fire protection systems all over the ship. On this warship with me was a guy named Dominique. Dominique was a squared-away sailor who worked down in the main engine room. He was an undesignated fireman. What that essentially means is he is assigned to the engineering department on the ship and when it's time for him to take the test to be E4, or third class petty officer he would do what is called strike a rate; simply put, picking a job. Dominique was interested in being a damage control man. Not only did he have his own responsibilities down in the main engineering room that he had to worry about, he had to set time aside to learn the damage control job as well. He was a constant presence in the damage control shop and we all knew he would be a great addition to our division. He worked hard to understand all the damage control systems on the ship, the repair lockers, the fire protection systems and more. He completed all of his personal qualification standards in basic damage control and more. I was drawn to him from the start. I could see the passion he had and his rock hard work ethic as soon as he walked up to the office and asked me and a couple others to help him learn the damage control rate. The time came for him to sit for his test and he passed with flying colors and was promoted to damage control man third class. He reported to the DC division and would work with me in what we call the systems shop. I did my best to try to provide him good leadership because I knew it was just a matter of time before he took my job and moved right up the ranks. Eventually that's exactly what he did. I would go on to take a test and become promoted and he would take my spot as a supervisor.

My time in the Navy was coming to a close. I was preparing to be separated and move into my career in the fire service. Dominique and I left the ship around the same time, but before we parted ways he said something that meant the world to me. He said, "I'm not sure where I'll be stationed or where you'll be either, but if I stay in the navy and I'm a chief I want you to pin my anchors on." I thought that was so cool. I told him I would absolutely do it and I didn't care where he was, I would be there. Almost 10 years went by since that conversation. One day, Dominique calls me up and he says, "Hey man I made chief, do you still want to pin my anchors on?" I couldn't be more excited. I was able to see Dominique as a young sailor working his butt off in the engineering space. I was able to see how much time and effort he put into becoming a damage control man, and a damn good one. Now I have the honor of pinning on one of his chief anchors on the back of the United States Navy destroyer. That was one of the greatest experiences I ever had. Right there next to me pinning his other anchor on was another one of our supervisors when we were all on the ship together. Somebody that mentored us, was hard on us, but taught us the importance of strong work ethic and looking out for your people. Thank you for everything Jimmy.

So why do I tell you that story? When I left that ship Dominique ran across many other great people, I'm sure. Plenty of other people I know would be deserving of pinning those anchors on his collar. But after all that time, he asked me. Now I guarantee Dominique can't tell you what awards I had or other commendations (he may remember the disciplinary stuff). He probably doesn't remember all the personal qualification standards I had to complete or maybe even what watch stations I was qualified in. There is one thing he does remember. He remembers the way people made him feel and what they taught him. He remembers the time we took out of our day to help him. He remembers what other did for him and his professional development as a young sailor.

What you do matters. Always remember that. I don't care how frustrated you grow at times, know that you have an important responsibility to mentor, coach, develop and take care of the people in your firehouse. You are their company officer, be their company officer. My goal was to offer you some substance that I hope you can take back to your firehouse and put into practice. I hope you were able to pull some nuggets from my experiences and provide the no-nonsense leadership that our firehouses need. Now, it's time to get out there and lead. Let's improve our organizations and our fire service as a whole one firehouse at a time! Good luck!

MY FINAL NUGGETS OF ADVICE

I have tried my best throughout this book to offer you some substance on realistic approaches to company officer leadership. I hope I have done that for you. In closing, I will lend you a short list of advice as you venture into your new role, or take a fresh look at the current role you are in.

1. Be yourself. They know who you were last week. Don't try to fool your crew. They know all about you already. Remember that credibility matters.

2. Look out for your crew. The right way! Look out for their morale, their development, and more. Look out for them, but don't be afraid to hold them accountable.

3. Address problems when they are small. Most big issues started out as small ones, but were ignored and continued to fester.

4. Speak the truth even if you have to choke on the

words. Speak the truth even if it's hard to get those words out. Do this to your crew and with your supervisors.

5. Work on building those relationships and establishing trust. Without trust, you have nothing. They must trust you with everything.

6. Set expectations. What you expect on the rig, around the station, and on calls. You can't hold them accountable to expectations that you haven't set.

7. Be quick to listen and slow to react. Always be in control of your emotions.

8. Train them and hold them to high standards.

9. Don't pre-judge people. Give everyone a chance. Give them the resources and help them get better, but don't sacrifice your values and where you want to take your team. You simply can't save them all and there will occasionally be some bad apples. Focus your energy on those who will move the team and organization forward.

10. You must be willing to accept loss. Maybe you have to remove someone from the team, it happens. It lets people know you have standards and shows them how committed you are to the team and your vision. Sometimes dead weight just needs to go.

11. Don't coddle people. Be empathetic, but don't coddle.

12. Be approachable

13. Don't be afraid to say I don't know.

14. Be a good manager of your time and theirs.

15. Give a damn even if others won't. Someone has to.

Lastly, above all else, lead by example. They will be watching.

Made in the USA
Middletown, DE
04 November 2022